ADVANCE PRAISE FOR *PERL ONE-LINERS*

"One of the slogans used by Perl is 'Easy things should be easy and hard things should be possible.' This book illustrates just how easy things can be—and how much can be done with so little code."
—David Precious, contributor to the Perl Dancer project and various CPAN modules

"By reading this book you can make a step toward becoming the local computer wizard, even without learning how to program."
—Gabor Szabo, founder and editor of the *Perl Weekly* newsletter

"A set of exercises for deepening your understanding of Perl."
—John D. Cook, Singular Value Consulting

"The author is enthusiastic about the material and uses an easy writing style. Highly recommended."
—Thrig (Jeremy Mates), Internet plumber

"These one-liners are great. Simple. Clear. Concise."
—Jonathan Scott Duff, Perl guru

"A quick read full of useful command-line Perl programs."
—Chris Fedde, systems engineer and Perl enthusiast

"Handy for anyone who does a lot of one-off text processing: system administrators, coders, or anyone with large amounts of data they need shifted, filtered, or interpreted."
—Jim Davis, Perl developer

PERL ONE-LINERS

PERL ONE-LINERS

130 Programs That Get Things Done

by Peteris Krumins

no starch press

San Francisco

Printed in USA
First printing

17 16 15 14 13   1 2 3 4 5 6 7 8 9

ISBN-10: 1-59327-520-X
ISBN-13: 978-1-59327-520-4

Publisher: William Pollock
Production Editor: Riley Hoffman
Cover Illustration: Tina Salameh
Interior Design: Octopod Studios
Developmental Editor: William Pollock
Technical Reviewer: Alastair McGowan-Douglas
Copyeditor: LeeAnn Pickrell
Compositor: Riley Hoffman
Proofreader: Elaine Merrill

For information on distribution, translations, or bulk sales, please contact No Starch Press, Inc. directly:

No Starch Press, Inc.
245 8th Street, San Francisco, CA 94103
phone: 415.863.9900; fax: 415.863.9950; info@nostarch.com; www.nostarch.com

Library of Congress Cataloging-in-Publication Data

```
Krumins, Peteris.
  Perl one-liners : 130 programs that get things done / by Peteris Krumins.
      pages cm
  Summary: "Snappy Perl programs to streamline tasks and sharpen coding skills"-- Provided by publisher.
   ISBN 978-1-59327-520-4 (paperback) -- ISBN 1-59327-520-X (paperback)
  1.  Perl (Computer program language)  I. Title.
  QA76.73.P22K78 2013
  005.13'3--dc23
                                      2013030613
```

About the Author

Peteris Krumins is a programmer, systems administrator, blogger, and all-around hacker. He is currently running his own company, Browserling, which focuses on cross-browser testing. He has self-published three books on essential UNIX tools, and he enjoys open-sourcing hundreds of small projects on GitHub.

 Find his website and blog at *http://www.catonmat.net/,* follow @pkrumins on Twitter, and see his open source projects at *http://github.com/pkrumins/.*

About the Technical Reviewer

Alastair McGowan-Douglas lives in Rugby in the UK. He has been a Perl developer since 2008 and is now stuck writing PHP for a living. His favorite pastime at work is writing Perl scripts for internal use to encourage others to embrace the language. Also a JavaScript developer and Git aficionado, his rantings and musings on these various subjects can be found at *http://altreus.blogspot.com/.*

BRIEF CONTENTS

CONTENTS IN DETAIL

4
CALCULATIONS

5
WORKING WITH ARRAYS AND STRINGS

6
TEXT CONVERSION AND SUBSTITUTION 59

7
SELECTIVELY PRINTING AND DELETING LINES 69

8
USEFUL REGULAR EXPRESSIONS   83

A
PERL'S SPECIAL VARIABLES   95

B
USING PERL ONE-LINERS ON WINDOWS   105

ACKNOWLEDGMENTS

I'd like to thank Eric Pement for inspiring me to write this book; Bill Pollock for giving me the opportunity to publish it at No Starch Press; Riley Hoffman and Laurel Chun for working with me to make it perfect; Alastair McGowan-Douglas for his technical review; and David Precious, Gabor Szabo, Jim Davis, Chris Fedde, Andy Lester, John D. Cook, Jonathan Scott Duff, and Jeremy Mates for reviewing the book and making great suggestions for improvements. I'd also like to thank everyone who helped me on the #perl IRC channel on freenode. If I forgot anyone, I'm sorry, but thanks for helping me to get this book written!

1

INTRODUCTION TO PERL ONE-LINERS

Perl one-liners are small and awesome Perl programs that fit in a single line of code. They do one thing really well—like changing line spacing, numbering lines, performing calculations, converting and substituting text, deleting and printing specific lines, parsing logs, editing files in-place, calculating statistics, carrying out system administration tasks, or updating a bunch of files at once. Perl one-liners will make you a shell warrior: what took you minutes (or even hours) to solve will now take you only seconds!

In this introductory chapter, I'll show you what one-liners look like and give you a taste of what's in the rest of the book. This book requires some Perl knowledge, but most of the one-liners can be tweaked and modified without knowing the language in depth.

Let's look at some examples. Here's one:

```
perl -pi -e 's/you/me/g' file
```

This one-liner replaces all occurrences of the text *you* with *me* in the file *file*. Very useful if you ask me. Imagine you're on a remote server and you need to replace text in a file. You can either open the file in a text editor and execute find-replace or simply perform the replacement through the command line and, bam, be done with it.

This one-liner and others in this book work well in UNIX. I'm using Perl 5.8 to run them, but they also work in newer Perl versions, such as Perl 5.10 and later. If you're on a Windows computer, you'll need to change them a little. To make this one-liner work on Windows, swap the single quotes for double quotes. To learn more about using Perl one-liners on Windows, see Appendix B.

I'll be using Perl's -e command-line argument throughout the book. It allows you to use the command line to specify the Perl code to be executed. In the previous one-liner, the code says "do the substitution (s/*you*/*me*/g command) and replace *you* with *me* globally (/g flag)." The -p argument ensures that the code is executed on every line of input and that the line is printed after execution. The -i argument ensures that *file* is edited in-place. Editing *in-place* means that Perl performs all the substitutions right in the file, overwriting the content you want to replace. I recommend that you always make a backup of the file you're working with by specifying the backup extension to the -i argument, like this:

```
perl -pi.bak -e 's/you/me/g' file
```

Now Perl creates a *file*.bak backup file first and only then changes the contents of *file*.

How about doing this same replacement in multiple files? Just specify the files on the command line:

```
perl -pi -e 's/you/me/g' file1 file2 file3
```

Here, Perl first replaces *you* with *me* in *file1* and then does the same in *file2* and *file3*.

You can also perform the same replacement only on lines that match *we*, as simply as this:

```
perl -pi -e 's/you/me/g if /we/' file
```

Here, you use the conditional if /*we*/ to ensure that s/*you*/*me*/g is executed only on lines that match the regular expression /*we*/.

The regular expression can be anything. Say you want to execute the substitution only on lines with digits in them. You could use the /\d/ regular expression to match numbers:

```
perl -pi -e 's/you/me/g if /\d/' file
```

How about finding all lines in a file that appear more than once?

```
perl -ne 'print if $a{$_}++' file
```

This one-liner records the lines you've seen so far in the %a hash and counts the number of times it sees the lines. If it has already seen the line, the condition $a{$_}++ is true, so it prints the line. Otherwise it "automagically" creates an element that contains the current line in the %a hash and increments its value. The $_ special variable contains the current line. This one-liner also uses the -n command-line argument to loop over the input, but unlike -p, it doesn't print the lines automatically. (Don't worry about all the command-line arguments right now; you'll learn about them as you work through this book!)

How about numbering lines? Super simple! Perl's $. special variable maintains the current line number. Just print it together with the line:

```
perl -ne 'print "$. $_"' file
```

You can do the same thing by using the -p argument and modifying the $_ variable:

```
perl -pe '$_ = "$. $_"' file
```

Here, each line is replaced by the string "$. $_", which is equal to the current line number followed by the line itself. (See one-liner 3.1 on page 17 for a full explanation.)

If you omit the filename at the end of the one-liner, Perl reads data from standard input. From now on, I'll assume the data comes from the standard input and drop the filename at the end. You can always put it back if you want to run one-liners on whole files.

You can also combine the previous two one-liners to create one that numbers only the repeated lines:

```
perl -ne 'print "$. $_" if $a{$_}++'
```

Another thing you can do is sum the numbers in each line using the sum function from the List::Util CPAN module. CPAN (Comprehensive Perl Archive Network; *http://www.cpan.org/*) is an archive of over 100,000 reusable Perl modules. List::Util is one of the modules on CPAN, and it contains various list utility functions. You don't need to install this module because it comes with Perl. (It's in Perl core.)

```
perl -MList::Util=sum -alne 'print sum @F'
```

The -MList::Util command-line argument imports the List::Util module. The =sum part of this one-liner imports the sum function from the List::Util module so that the program can use the function. Next, -a enables the automatic splitting of the current line into fields in the @F array. The splitting happens on the whitespace character by default. The -l argument ensures that print outputs a newline at the end of each line. Finally, sum @F sums all the elements in the @F list, and print prints the result followed by a newline (which I added with the -l argument). (See one-liner 4.2 on page 30 for a more detailed explanation.)

How about finding the date 1299 days ago? Try this:

```
perl -MPOSIX -le
  '@t = localtime; $t[3] -= 1299; print scalar localtime mktime @t'
```

I explain this example in detail in one-liner 4.19 (page 41), but basically you modify the fourth element of the structure returned by localtime, which happens to be days. You simply subtract 1299 days from the current day and then reassemble the result into a new time with localtime mktime @t and print the result in the scalar context to display human-readable time.

How about generating an eight-letter password? Here you go:

```
perl -le 'print map { ("a".."z")[rand 26] } 1..8'
```

The "a".."z" generates a list of letters from *a* to *z* (for a total of 26 letters). Then you randomly choose a letter eight times! (This example is explained in detail in one-liner 5.4 on page 51.)

Or suppose you want to find the decimal number that corresponds to an IP address. You can use unpack to find it really quickly:

```
perl -le 'print unpack("N", 127.0.0.1)'
```

This one-liner uses a *v-string*, which is a version literal. V-strings offer a way to compose a string with the specified ordinals. The IP address 127.0.0.1 is treated as a v-string, meaning the numbers 127, 0, 0, 1 are concatenated together into a string of four characters, where the first character has ordinal value 127, the second and third characters have ordinal values 0, and the last character has ordinal value 1. Next, unpack unpacks them to a single decimal number in "network" (big-endian) order. (See one-liner 4.27 on page 45 for more.)

What about calculations? Let's find the sum of the numbers in the first column in a table:

```
perl -lane '$sum += $F[0]; END { print $sum }'
```

The lines are automatically split into fields with the -a argument, which can be accessed through the @F array. The first element of the array, $F[0], is the first column, so you simply sum all the columns with $sum += $F[0]. When the Perl program finishes, it executes any code in the END block, which, in this case, prints the total sum. Easy!

Now let's find out how many packets have passed through iptables rules:

```
iptables -L -nvx | perl -lane '$pkts += $F[0]; END { print $pkts }'
```

The iptables program outputs the packets in the first column. All you have to do to find out how many packets have passed through the firewall rules is sum the numbers in the first column. Although iptables will output table headers as well, you can safely ignore these because Perl converts them to zero for the += operation.

How about getting a list of all users on the system?

```
perl -a -F: -lne 'print $F[4]' /etc/passwd
```

Combining -a with the -F argument lets you specify the character where lines should be split, which, by default, is whitespace. Here, you split lines on the colon character, the record separator of /etc/passwd. Next, you print the fifth field, $F[4], which contains the user's real name.

If you ever get lost with command-line arguments, remember that Perl comes with a fantastic documentation system called *perldoc*. Type **perldoc perlrun** at the command line. This will display the documentation about how to run Perl and all the command-line arguments. It's very useful when you suddenly forget which command-line argument does what and need to look it up quickly. You may also want to read *perldoc perlvar*, which explains variables; *perldoc perlop*, which explains operators; and *perldoc perlfunc*, which explains functions.

Perl one-liners let you accomplish many tasks quickly. You'll find over 130 one-liners in this book. Read them, try them, and soon enough you'll be the local shell wizard. (Just don't tell your friends—unless you want competition.)

Enjoy!

2

SPACING

In this chapter, we look at various one-liners that change line and word spacing, performing such tasks as double- and triple-spacing lines in a file, removing blank lines, and double-spacing words. You'll also learn about various command-line arguments, such as -p, -e, -n, and special variables, such as $_ and $\.

2.1   Double-space a file

```
perl -pe '$\ = "\n"' file
```

This one-liner double-spaces a file. I need to explain three things here: the -p and -e command-line options and the short $\ = "\n" Perl program.

Use the -e option to enter a Perl program directly at the command line. Typically you won't want to create source files for every small program; with -e you can easily write a program directly at the command line as a one-liner. In this case, the entire Perl program contained in this one-liner is $\ = "\n". Be sure to use single quotes (') around the program, or your shell will interpret things like $\ as shell variables, which have no value, effectively removing them!

Now let's look at the -p switch. Specifying -p tells Perl to assume the following loop around your program:

```
while (<>) {
    # your program goes here (specified by -e)
} continue {
    print or die "-p failed: $!\n";
}
```

Broadly speaking, this construct loops over all the input, executes your code, and prints the value of $_ (the print statement prints the value of $_), which allows you to modify all or some lines of the input quickly. The $_ variable is a special variable that gets replaced with the current line of text. It can be replaced with other stuff as well. You'll learn all about $_ as you work through the book. (See Appendix A for a summary of its use cases.)

But understanding what is going on in this loop in more detail is important. First, the while (<>) loop takes each line from the standard input and puts it in the $_ variable. Next, the code specified by -e is executed, followed by the print or die portion.

The continue statement executes the print or die statement after each line, which attempts to print the contents of the $_ variable. If the attempt fails (for example, the terminal is not writable or standard output has been redirected to something that isn't writable), die makes Perl exit (die) with an error message.

In this one-liner, the code specified by -e is $\ = "\n", so the program that Perl executes looks like this:

```
while (<>) {
    $\ = "\n";
} continue {
    print or die "-p failed: $!\n";
}
```

This Perl program reads each line into the $_ variable and then sets $\ to a newline and calls print. Another special variable is $\. It is similar to the ORS (Output Record Separator) variable in Awk in that it is appended after every print operation. A print statement with no arguments prints the contents of $_ and appends $\ at the end of the output.

As a result, each line is printed unmodified, followed by the $\, which was set to newline. The input is now double-spaced.

In fact, you actually do not need to set $\ to newline for every line; you can set it just once at the beginning of the program:

```
perl -pe 'BEGIN { $\ = "\n" }' file
```

This one-liner sets $\ to the newline character just once before Perl does anything in the BEGIN code block. The BEGIN block is a special code block that is executed before everything else in a Perl program. Here's what the expanded Perl program looks like, and it works exactly the same way as the previous one-liner:

```
BEGIN { $\ = "\n" }

while (<>) {
} continue {
    print or die "-p failed: $!\n";
}
```

Here is another way to double-space a file. This one-liner appends another newline character at the end of each line and then prints the line:

```
perl -pe '$_ .= "\n"' file
```

This one-liner is equivalent to

```
while (<>) {
    $_ = $_ . "\n"
} continue {
    print or die "-p failed: $!\n";
}
```

Writing $_ = $_ . "\n" is the same as writing $_ .= "\n". This expression simply concatenates $_ with "\n". (The period (.) is the string concatenation operator.)

But probably the cleanest way to double-space a file is to use the substitution operator s:

```
perl -pe 's/$/\n/' file
```

This one-liner replaces the regular expression $ that matches the end of a line with a newline, effectively adding a newline at the end.

If you're running Perl 5.10 or later, you can use the say operator. The say operator acts much like print, but it always adds a newline at the end of the line. In Perl 5.10, this same one-liner can be written like this:

```
perl -nE 'say' file
```

The -E command-line argument works exactly the same way as the -e command-line argument, but it also enables Perl 5.10 features, including the say operator. The -n argument is similar to -p, but you have to print the line yourself. (I explain the -n argument in more detail in one-liner 2.6.) This one-liner prints the line, followed by another newline that's appended by the say operator.

For example, if a file contains four lines:

```
line1
line2
line3
line4
```

running any of these one-liners outputs the following:

```
line1

line2

line3

line4
```

In these first few examples, I passed a filename as the last argument to the one-liners. When I do that, the one-liners operate on the contents of that file. If I didn't pass a filename to the one-liners, they'd operate on the data from the standard input. From now on I won't specify a file at the end of the one-liners, but you can always add it back if you want to run the one-liners on files. When writing one-liners, it's a good idea to quickly test if they're correct by typing something directly to the standard input. Then when you're sure the one-liner works, you can pass one or more filenames at the end.

Again, don't forget about Perl's handy documentation system, *perldoc*. Just type **perldoc perlrun** at the command line to display information about how to run Perl and all the command-line arguments.

2.2 Double-space a file, excluding the blank lines

```
perl -pe '$_ .= "\n" unless /^$/'
```

This one-liner double-spaces all lines that are not completely empty by appending a newline character at the end of each nonblank line. The unless means "if not," and unless /^$/ means "if not 'beginning then end of line.'" The condition "beginning then end of line" is true only for blank lines.

Here's how this one-liner looks when expanded:

```
while (<>) {
    unless (/^$/) {
        $_ .= "\n"
    }
} continue {
    print or die "-p failed: $!\n";
}
```

Here is a better test, which takes into account spaces and tabs on a line:

```
perl -pe '$_ .= "\n" if /\S/'
```

Here, the line is matched against \S—a regular expression sequence that is the inverse of \s, which matches any whitespace character (including tab, vertical tab, space, newline, and carriage return). The inverse of \s is any nonwhitespace character. The result is that every line with at least one nonwhitespace character is double-spaced.

2.3 Triple-space a file

You can also triple-space a file simply by outputting more newlines at the end of each line:

```
perl -pe '$\ = "\n\n"'
```

Or

```
perl -pe '$_ .= "\n\n"'
```

Or

```
perl -pe 's/$/\n\n/'
```

These one-liners are similar to the first one-liner in this chapter, except that two newlines are appended after each line.

2.4   N-space a file

```
perl -pe '$_ .= "\n"x7'
```

This one-liner inserts seven newlines after each line. Notice how I've used "\n" x 7 to repeat the newline character seven times. The x operator repeats the value on the left *N* times.

For example, the line

```
perl -e 'print "foo"x5'
```

prints foofoofoofoofoo.

As a side note, sometimes when you need to generate a certain amount of data, the x operator comes in really handy. For example, to generate 1KB of data, you could do this:

```
perl -e 'print "a"x1024'
```

This one-liner prints the *a* character 1024 times.

2.5   Add a blank line before every line

```
perl -pe 's/^/\n/'
```

This one-liner uses the s/*regex*/*replace*/ operator. It substitutes the given regular expression with the replacement. In this one-liner, the operator is s/^/\n/, the regular expression is ^, and the replacement is \n. The ^ pattern matches the beginning position of the text, and the s operator replaces it with \n, a newline. As a result, the newline character is inserted before the line. To insert something else before the line, simply replace \n with the bit to be inserted.

2.6   Remove all blank lines

```
perl -ne 'print unless /^$/'
```

This one-liner uses the -n flag, which tells Perl to assume a different loop, other than -p, around the program:

```
while (<>) {
    # your program goes here
}
```

Compare this loop to the one that Perl assumes when you specify -p, and you'll see that this loop has no continue { print or die } part. In this loop, each line is read by the diamond operator <> and is placed in the special variable $_, but it's not printed! You have to print the line yourself—a useful feature if you want to print, modify, or delete lines selectively.

In this one-liner, the code is print unless /^$/, so the entire Perl program becomes

```
while (<>) {
    print unless /^$/
}
```

Unraveling this a bit further, you get this:

```
while (<>) {
    print $_ unless $_ =~ /^$/
}
```

This one-liner prints all nonblank lines. (You saw the /^$/ regular expression in one-liner 2.2 on page 11.)

This one-liner also removes all blank lines:

```
perl -lne 'print if length'
```

This one-liner uses the -l command-line argument, which automatically chomps the input line (basically removes the newline at the end) and appends it back at the end of the line when printing. The code specified to the -e argument is 'print if length', which says "print the line if it has some length." Empty lines have a length of 0, so they're not printed (0 is a false value in Perl, so the if length condition evaluates to false). All other lines have length and are printed. Without -l, the string would still have the newline at the end and thus be 1 or 2 characters long![1]

Here's another one-liner to remove all blank lines:

```
perl -ne 'print if /\S/'
```

This one-liner behaves slightly differently from the previous two. Both print unless /^$/ and print if length also print the lines that consist of only spaces and/or tabs. Such lines appear to be empty to the eye, and you may want to filter them. This one-liner uses \S (explained in one-liner 2.2 on page 11), a regular expression sequence that matches nonblank characters. Lines containing only spaces and/or tabs don't match \S and therefore are not printed.

---

1. Windows uses two characters for the newline.

As you can see, you can write the same program in many different ways. In fact, Perl's motto is *There's More Than One Way To Do It*, which is abbreviated as *TIMTOWTDI* and pronounced "Tim Toady." (Fun trivia: Larry Wall, the inventor of Perl, uses the handle @TimToady on Twitter and IRC.)

2.7   Remove all consecutive blank lines, leaving only one

```
perl -00 -pe ''
```

This one-liner is really tricky, isn't it? First, it doesn't have any code! The -e is empty. Next, it has a silly -00 command-line option that turns *paragraph slurp mode* on, meaning Perl reads text paragraph by paragraph, rather than line by line. (A paragraph is text between two or more newlines.) The paragraph is put into $_, and the -p option prints it out.

You can even write this in a shorter fashion:

```
perl -00pe0
```

Here, the code specified to -e is 0, which does nothing.

This is one of my favorite one-liners because if you haven't seen it before, it can be tricky to figure out, and I love mind games. (There's no code specified to -e! How can it possibly do something?)

2.8   Compress/expand all blank lines into N consecutive lines

Say you have a file with two blank lines after each paragraph, and you wish to expand the line spacing between the paragraphs to three lines. To do so, you can simply combine one-liners 2.4 and 2.7 like this:

```
perl -00 -pe '$_ .= "\n"x2'
```

This one-liner slurps lines paragraph-wise via the -00 option and then appends three newline characters after each paragraph. The code "\n"x2 prints two newlines, which are added to the blank line already at the end of the paragraph.

In a similar vein, you can also reduce the spacing between paragraphs. Say you've got a file that for some crazy reason has ten blank lines between paragraphs, and you want to compress these blank lines to just three. You can use the same one-liner again!

2.9   Double-space between all words

```
perl -pe 's/ /  /g'
```

Here, you use the substitution operator s to replace one space " " with two spaces " " globally on each line (the /g flag makes the replacement global), and you're done. It's that simple!

Here's an example. Let's say you have this line of text:

```
this line doesn't have enough whitespace!
```

Running this one-liner increases the spacing between words:

```
this  line  doesn't  have  enough  whitespace!
```

2.10   Remove all spacing between words

```
perl -pe 's/ +//g'
```

This one-liner uses the " +" regular expression to match one or more spaces. When it finds a match, it substitutes it with nothing, globally, which deletes all spaces between words.

If you also want to get rid of tabs and other special characters that might add spacing, use the \s+ regular expression, which means "match a space, a tab, a vertical tab, a newline, or a carriage return":

```
perl -pe 's/\s+//g'
```

Here's an example. Let's say you have this line of text:

```
this line has too much whitespace said cowboy neal
```

Running this one-liner removes all spaces:

```
thislinehastoomuchwhitespacesaidcowboyneal
```

2.11 Change all spacing between words to one space

```
perl -pe 's/ +/ /g'
```

This one-liner is similar to the previous one, except that it replaces one or more spaces with just one space.

For example, if you have this line:

```
this    line has really        messed-up                spacing
```

running this one-liner normalizes the spacing between words to one space:

```
this line has really messed-up spacing
```

2.12 Insert a space between all characters

```
perl -lpe 's// /g'
```

Here you match seemingly nothing and replace it with a single space. The nothingness actually means "match between characters," with the result that you insert a space between all characters. (The matching includes the beginning and end of the text.)

For example, given this line:

```
today was a great day
```

running this one-liner produces this result:

```
 t o d a y   w a s   a   g r e a t   d a y
```

It might be difficult to see where all the spaces are added, so let's illustrate that by modifying this one-liner to insert a colon between all characters:

```
perl -lpe 's//:/g'
```

This will output:

```
:t:o:d:a:y: :w:a:s: :a: :g:r:e:a:t: :d:a:y:
```

As you can see, spaces (or colons) are also inserted at the beginning and end of the text. Also note that the existing spaces count as characters, so they're triple-spaced.

3

NUMBERING

In this chapter, we'll look at various one-liners for numbering lines and words, and you'll get to know the $.$ special variable. You'll also learn about Perl golfing, a "sport" that involves writing the shortest Perl program to get a task done.

3.1   Number all lines in a file

```
perl -pe '$_ = "$. $_"'
```

As I explained in one-liner 2.1 (page 7), -p tells Perl to assume a loop around the program (specified by -e) that reads each line of input into the $_ variable, executes the program, and then prints the contents of the $_ variable.

This one-liner simply modifies $_ by prepending the $. variable to it. The special variable $. contains the current line number of the input. The result is that each line has its line number prepended.

Similarly, you can also use the -n argument and print the string "$. $_", which is the current line number followed by the line:

```
perl -ne 'print "$. $_"'
```

Say a file contains three lines:

```
foo
bar
baz
```

Running this one-liner numbers them:

```
1 foo
2 bar
3 baz
```

3.2   Number only non-empty lines in a file

```
perl -pe '$_ = ++$x." $_" if /./'
```

Here you employ an "action if condition" statement that executes an action only if the condition is true. In this case, the condition is the regular expression /./, which matches all characters other than newline (that is, it matches a non-empty line). The action $_ = ++$x." $_" prepends the variable $x incremented by one to the current line. Because you're not using the strict pragma, $x is created automatically the first time it's incremented.

The result is that at each non-empty line $x is incremented by one and prepended to that line. Nothing is modified at the empty lines, and they are printed as is.

One-liner 2.2 (page 11) shows another way to match non-empty lines through the \S regular expression:

```
perl -pe '$_ = ++$x." $_" if /\S/'
```

Say a file contains four lines, two of which are empty:

```
line1

line4
```

Running this one-liner numbers only lines one and four:

```
1 line1

2 line4
```

3.3   Number and print only non-empty lines in a file (drop empty lines)

```
perl -ne 'print ++$x." $_" if /./'
```

This one-liner uses the -n program argument, which places the line in the $_ variable and then executes the program specified by -e. Unlike -p, -n does not print the line after executing the code in -e, so you have to call print explicitly to print the contents of the $_ variable.

The one-liner calls print only on lines with at least one character, and as in the previous one-liner, it increments the line number in the variable $x by one for each non-empty line. The empty lines are ignored and never printed.

Say a file contains the same four lines as in one-liner 3.2:

```
line1

line4
```

Running this one-liner drops the empty lines and numbers lines one and four:

```
1 line1
2 line4
```

3.4 Number all lines but print line numbers only for non-empty lines

```
perl -pe '$_ = "$. $_" if /./'
```

This one-liner is similar to one-liner 3.2. Here, you modify the $_ variable that holds the entire line only if the line has at least one character. All other empty lines are printed as is, without line numbers.

Say a file contains four lines:

```
line1


line4
```

Running this one-liner numbers all the lines but prints the line numbers only for lines one and four:

```
1 line1


4 line4
```

3.5 Number only lines that match a pattern; print others unmodified

```
perl -pe '$_ = ++$x." $_" if /regex/'
```

Here, again, you use an "action if condition" statement, and again the condition is a pattern (a regular expression): /regex/. The action is the same as in one-liner 3.2.

Say a file contains these lines:

```
record foo
bar baz
record qux
```

and you want to number the lines that contain the word *record*. You can replace /regex/ in the one-liner with /record/:

```
perl -pe '$_ = ++$x." $_" if /record/'
```

When you run this one-liner, it gives you the following output:

```
1 record foo
bar baz
2 record qux
```

3.6   Number and print only lines that match a pattern

```
perl -ne 'print ++$x." $_" if /regex/'
```

This one-liner is almost exactly like one-liner 3.3, except it only numbers and prints lines that match /regex/. It doesn't print nonmatching lines.

For example, a file contains the same lines as in one-liner 3.5:

```
record foo
bar baz
record qux
```

And let's say you want to number and print only the lines that contain the word *record*. In this case, changing /regex/ to /record/ and running the one-liner gives you this result:

```
1 record foo
2 record qux
```

3.7   Number all lines but print line numbers only for lines that match a pattern

```
perl -pe '$_ = "$. $_" if /regex/'
```

This one-liner is similar to one-liners 3.4 and 3.6. Here, the line number is prepended to the line if the line matches a /regex/; otherwise, it's simply printed without a line number.

Replacing /regex/ with /record/ and running this one-liner on the same example file shown in one-liner 3.6 gives you this output:

```
1 record foo
bar baz
3 record qux
```

3.8   Number all lines in a file using a custom format

```
perl -ne 'printf "%-5d %s", $., $_'
```

This one-liner uses `printf` to print the line number together with the line contents. `printf` does formatted printing. You specify the format and send it the data to print, and it formats and prints the data accordingly. Here, the format for the line numbers is `%-5d`, which aligns the line numbers five positions to the left.

Here's an example. Say the input to this one-liner is

```
hello world
bye world
```

Then the output is

```
1     hello world
2     bye world
```

Other format strings include `%5d`, which aligns the line numbers five positions to the right, and `%05d`, which zero-fills and right-justifies the line numbers. Here's the output you get with the `%5d` format string for line numbers:

```
    1 hello world
    2 bye world
```

And this is what you get with the `%05d` format string:

```
00001 hello world
00002 bye world
```

To learn more about the various formats that are available, run **perldoc -f sprintf** at the command line.

3.9   Print the total number of lines in a file (emulate wc -l)

```
perl -lne 'END { print $. }'
```

This one-liner uses the `END` block that Perl took as a feature from the Awk language. The `END` block is executed once the Perl program has executed. Here, the Perl program is the hidden loop over the input created by the -n argument. Once it loops over the input, the special variable $. contains the number of lines in the input, and the END block prints this variable. The -l parameter sets the output record separator for print to a newline, so you don't have to print the newline yourself, like this: print "$.\n".

You can do the same thing with this one-liner:

```
perl -le 'print $n = () = <>'
```

This one-liner is easy to grasp if you understand Perl contexts well. The () = <> part tells Perl to evaluate the <> operator (the *diamond operator*) in the list context, which makes the diamond operator read the whole file as a list of lines. Next, you assign this list to $n. Because $n is scalar, this list assignment is evaluated in the scalar context.

What's really happening here is the = operator is right-associative, meaning the = on the right is done first and the = on the left is done second:

```
perl -le 'print $n = (() = <>)'
```

Evaluating a list assignment in the scalar context returns the number of elements in the list; thus, the $n = () = <> construction is equal to the number of lines in the input, that is, the number of lines in the file. The print statement prints this number. The -l argument ensures a newline is added after printing this number.

You can also drop the variable $n from this one-liner and force the scalar context through the scalar operator:

```
perl -le 'print scalar(() = <>)'
```

Here, instead of evaluating a list assignment in the scalar context by assigning it again to another scalar, you simply evaluate the list assignment in the scalar context using the scalar operator.

And now for a more obvious version:

```
perl -le 'print scalar(@foo = <>)'
```

Here, instead of using an empty list () to force the list context on <>, you use the variable @foo to achieve the same effect.

And here's another way to do it:

```
perl -ne '}{print $.'
```

This one-liner uses the so-called *eskimo operator* }{ (actually a clever construct) in conjunction with the -n command-line argument. As I explained earlier, the -n argument forces Perl to assume a while(<>) { }

loop around the program. The eskimo operator forces Perl to escape the loop, and the one-liner expands to

```
while (<>) {
}{                    # eskimo operator here
    print $.;
}
```

As you can see, this program just loops over all the input, and once it's finished, it prints the $., which is the number of lines in the input. It becomes even more obvious if you change the formatting a little:

```
while (<>) {}

{
    print $.;
}
```

As you can see, this is just an empty loop that loops over all the input, followed by the print statement wrapped in curly brackets.

3.10 Print the number of non-empty lines in a file

```
perl -le 'print scalar(grep { /./ } <>)'
```

This one-liner uses Perl's grep function, which is similar to the grep UNIX command. Given a list of values, grep { condition } list returns only those values in the list that make the condition true. In this case, the condition is a regular expression that matches at least one character, so the input is filtered and grep{ /./ } returns all non-empty lines. To get the number of lines, you evaluate grep in the scalar context and print the result.

Some Perl programmers like to create the shortest Perl program that does some particular task—an exercise called *Perl golfing*. A golfer's version of this one-liner would replace scalar() with ~~ (double bitwise negate) and drop the spaces, shortening it like this:

```
perl -le 'print ~~grep{/./}<>'
```

This double bitwise negate trick is effectively a synonym for scalar because the bitwise negation works on scalar values, so grep is evaluated in the scalar context.

You can make this even shorter by dropping the space after print and getting rid of the curly brackets:

```
perl -le 'print~~grep/./,<>'
```

If you have Perl 5.10 or later, you can also use the -E command-line switch and the say operator:

```
perl -lE 'say~~grep/./,<>'
```

A true golfer's masterpiece!

3.11 Print the number of empty lines in a file

```
perl -lne '$x++ if /^$/; END { print $x+0 }'
```

Here, you use the variable $x to count the number of empty lines encountered. Once you've looped over all the lines, you print the value of $x in the END block. You use the $x+0 construction to ensure that 0 is output if no lines are empty. (Otherwise $x is never created and is undefined. Adding +0 to the undefined value produces 0.) An alternative to $x+0 is the int operator:

```
perl -lne '$x++ if /^$/; END { print int $x }'
```

You could also modify the previous one-liner by doing this:

```
perl -le 'print scalar(grep { /^$/ } <>)'
```

Or write it with ~~:

```
perl -le 'print ~~grep{ /^$/ } <>'
```

The ~~ does bitwise negation twice, which makes grep execute in the scalar context and return the number of empty lines.

These last two versions are not as effective as the one-liner with the END block because they read the whole file into memory, whereas the one-liner with the END block does it line by line and, therefore, keeps only one line of input in memory.

3.12 Print the number of lines in a file that match a pattern (emulate grep -c)

```
perl -lne '$x++ if /regex/; END { print $x+0 }'
```

This one-liner is basically the same as 3.11, except it increments the line counter $x by one when a line matches the regular expression /regex/. The $x+0 trick makes sure 0 is printed when no lines match /regex/. (See one-liner 3.11 for a more detailed explanation of the $x+0 trick.)

3.13   Number words across all lines

```
perl -pe 's/(\w+)/++$i.".$1"/ge'
```

This one-liner uses the /e flag, which makes Perl evaluate the *replace* part of the s/*regex*/*replace*/ expression as code!

The code here is ++$i.".$1", which means "increment variable $i by one and then add it in front of the string ".$1" (that is, a dot followed by the contents of the matched group $1)." The matched group here is each word: (\w+).

In one sentence, this one-liner matches a word (\w+), puts it in $1, and then executes the ++$i.".$1" code that numbers the word globally (/g flag). There—all words are numbered.

For example, if you have a file with the following three lines:

```
just another
perl hacker
hacking perl code
```

running this one-liner numbers each word in the file and produces the following output:

```
1.just 2.another
3.perl 4.hacker
5.hacking 6.perl 7.code
```

3.14   Number words on each individual line

```
perl -pe '$i=0; s/(\w+)/++$i.".$1"/ge'
```

This is similar to one-liner 3.13, except that you reset the $i variable to 0 on each line. Here's the result of running this one-liner on the example from one-liner 3.13:

```
1.just 2.another
1.perl 2.hacker
1.hacking 2.perl 3.code
```

As you can see, in each line the words are numbered independently of other lines.

3.15 Replace all words with their numeric positions

```
perl -pe 's/(\w+)/++$i/ge'
```

This one-liner is almost the same as one-liner 3.13. Here, you simply replace each word with its numeric position, which is kept in the variable $i. For example, if you run this one-liner on the file from one-liners 3.13 and 3.14, it replaces the words in the file with their numeric positions to produce this output:

```
1 2
3 4
5 6 7
```

Fun!

4

CALCULATIONS

In this chapter, we'll look at various one-liners for performing calculations, such as finding minimum and maximum elements, counting, shuffling and permuting words, and calculating dates and numbers. You'll also learn about the -a, -M, and -F command-line arguments, the $, special variable, and the @{[...]} construction that lets you run code inside double quotes.

4.1   Check if a number is a prime

```
perl -lne '(1x$_) !~ /^1?$|^(11+?)\1+$/ && print "$_ is prime"'
```

This one-liner uses an ingenious regular expression by Abigail to detect whether a given number is a prime. (Don't take this regular expression too seriously; I've included it for its artistic value. For serious purposes, use the Math::Primality module from CPAN to see whether a number is prime.)

Here's how this ingenious one-liner works: First, the number is converted into its unary representation by (1x$_). For example, 5 is converted into 1x5, which is 11111 (1 repeated 5 times). Next, the unary number is tested against the regular expression. If it doesn't match, the number is a prime; otherwise it's a composite. The !~ operator is the opposite of the =~ operator and is true if the regular expression doesn't match.

The regular expression consists of two parts: The first part, ^1?$, matches 1 and the empty string. The empty string and 1 are clearly not prime numbers, so this part of the regular expression discards them.

The second part, ^(11+?)\1+$, determines whether two or more 1s repeatedly make up the whole number. If so, the regular expression matches, which means the number is a composite. If not, it's a prime.

Now consider how the second part of the regular expression would act on the number 5. The number 5 in unary is 11111, so the (11+?) matches the first two 1s, the back-reference \1 becomes 11, and the whole regular expression now becomes ^11(11)+$. Because it can't match five 1s, it fails. Next, it attempts to match the first three 1s. The back-reference becomes 111, and the whole regular expression becomes ^111(111)+$, which doesn't match. The process repeats for 1111 and 11111, which also don't match, and as a result the entire regular expression doesn't match and the number is a prime.

What about the number 4? The number 4 is 1111 in unary. The (11+?) matches the first two 1s. The back-reference \1 becomes 11, and the regular expression becomes ^11(11)+$, which matches the original string and confirms that the number is not prime.

4.2   Print the sum of all fields on each line

```
perl -MList::Util=sum -alne 'print sum @F'
```

This one-liner turns on field *auto-splitting* with the -a command-line option and imports the sum function from the List::Util module with -Mlist::Util=sum. (List::Util is part of the Perl core, so you don't need install it.) Auto-splitting happens on whitespace characters by default, and the resulting fields are put in the @F variable. For example, the line 1 4 8 would be split on each space so that @F would become (1, 4, 8). The sum @F statement sums the elements in the @F array, giving you 13.

The -Mmodule=arg option imports arg from module. It's the same as writing

```
use module qw(arg);
```

This one-liner is equivalent to

```
use List::Util qw(sum);
while (<>) {
    @F = split(' ');
    print sum @F, "\n";
}
```

You can change auto-splitting's default behavior by specifying an argument to the -F command-line switch. Say you have the following line:

```
1:2:3:4:5:6:7:8:9:10
```

And you wish to find the sum of all these numbers. You can simply specify : as an argument to the -F switch, like this:

```
perl -MList::Util=sum -F: -alne 'print sum @F'
```

This splits the line on the colon character and sums all the numbers. The output is 55 because that's the sum of the numbers 1 through 10.

4.3 Print the sum of all fields on all lines

```
perl -MList::Util=sum -alne 'push @S,@F; END { print sum @S }'
```

This one-liner keeps pushing the split fields in @F to the @S array. Once the input stops and Perl is about to quit, the END { } block is executed and it outputs the sum of all items in @F. This sums all fields over all lines.

Notice how pushing the @F array to the @S array actually appends elements to it. This differs from many other languages, where pushing array1 to array2 would put array1 into array2, rather than appending the elements of array1 onto array2. Perl performs list flattening by design.

Unfortunately, summing all fields on all lines using this solution creates a massive @S array. A better solution is to keep only the running sum, like this:

```
perl -MList::Util=sum -alne '$s += sum @F; END { print $s }'
```

Here, each line is split into @F and the values are summed and stored in the running sum variable $s. Once all input has been processed, the one-liner prints the value of $s.

4.4   Shuffle all fields on each line

```
perl -MList::Util=shuffle -alne 'print "@{[shuffle @F]}"'
```

The trickiest part of this one-liner is the @{[shuffle @F]} construction. This construction allows you to execute the code inside the quotation marks. Normally text and variables are placed inside quotation marks, but with the @{[...]} construction you can run code, too.

In this one-liner, the code to execute inside of the quotation marks is shuffle @F, which shuffles the fields and returns the shuffled list. The [shuffle @F] creates an array reference containing the shuffled fields, and the @{ ... } dereferences it. You simply create a reference and immediately dereference it. This allows you to run the code inside the quotation marks.

Let's look at several examples to understand why I chose to run the code inside the quotation marks. If I had written print shuffle @F, the fields on the line would be concatenated. Compare the output of this one-liner:

```
$ echo a b c d | perl -MList::Util=shuffle -alne 'print "@{[shuffle @F]}"'
b c d a
```

to this:

```
$ echo a b c d | perl -MList::Util=shuffle -alne 'print shuffle @F'
bcda
```

In the first example, the array of shuffled fields (inside the double quotation marks) is interpolated, and the array's elements are separated by a space, so the output is b c d a. In the second example, interpolation doesn't happen, and Perl simply dumps out element by element without separating them, and the output is bcda.

You can use the $, special variable to change the separator between array elements when they're printed. For example, here's what happens when I change the separator to a colon:

```
$ echo a b c d | perl -MList::Util=shuffle -alne '$,=":"; print shuffle @F'
b:c:d:a
```

You can also use the `join` function to join the elements of `@F` with a space:

```
perl -MList::Util=shuffle -alne 'print join " ", shuffle @F'
```

Here, the `join` function joins the elements of an array using the given separator, but the `@{[ ... ]}` construction is the cleanest way to do it.

4.5   Find the numerically smallest element (minimum element) on each line

```
perl -MList::Util=min -alne 'print min @F'
```

This one-liner is somewhat similar to the previous ones. It uses the `min` function from `List::Util`. Once the line has been automatically split by `-a` and the elements are in the `@F` array, the `min` function finds the numerically smallest element, which it prints.

For example, if you have a file that contains these lines:

```
-8   9   10 5
7    0   9  3
5   -25  9  999
```

Running this one-liner produces the following output:

```
-8
0
-25
```

The smallest number on the first line is `-8`; on the second line, the smallest number is `0`; and on the third line, `-25`.

4.6   Find the numerically smallest element (minimum element) over all lines

```
perl -MList::Util=min -alne '@M = (@M, @F); END { print min @M }'
```

This one-liner combines one-liners 4.3 and 4.5. The `@M = (@M, @F)` construct is the same as `push @M, @F`. It appends the contents of `@F` to the `@M` array.

This one-liner stores all data in memory, and if you run it on a really huge file, Perl will run out of memory. Your best bet is to find the smallest element on every line and compare that element with the smallest element on the previous line. If the element on the current line is less than the previous one, it's the smallest element so far. Once all lines have been processed, you can just print the smallest element found through the END block:

```
perl -MList::Util=min -alne '
  $min = min @F;
  $rmin = $min unless defined $rmin && $min > $rmin;
  END { print $rmin }
'
```

Here, you first find the minimum element on the current line and store it in $min. Then you check to see if the smallest element on the current line is the smallest element so far. If so, assign it to $rmin. Once you've looped over the whole input, the END block executes and you print the $rmin.

Say your file contains these lines:

```
-8  9  10 5
7   0  9  3
5  -25 9  999
```

Running this one-liner outputs -25 because that's the smallest number in the file.

If you're using Perl 5.10 or later, you can do the same thing with this one-liner:

```
perl -MList::Util=min -alne '$min = min($min // (), @F); END { print $min }'
```

This one-liner uses the // operator, which is new to Perl 5.10. This operator is similar to the logical OR operator (||), except that it tests the left side's definedness rather than the truth. What that means is it tests whether the left side is defined rather than whether it is true or false. In this one-liner, the expression $min // () returns $min if $min has been defined, or else it returns an empty list (). The // operator saves you from having to use defined to test definedness.

Consider what happens when this one-liner is run on the previous file. First, Perl reads the line -8 9 10 5 , splits it, and puts the numbers in the @F array. The @F array is now (-8, 9, 10, 5). Next, it executes $min = min ($min // (), @F). Because $min hasn't been defined, $min // () evaluates to (), so the whole expression becomes $min = min ((), (-8, 9, 10, 5)).

Perl does list flattening by design, so after flattening the arguments to the min function, the expression becomes $min = min(-8, 9, 10, 5). This defines $min, setting it to -8. Perl proceeds to the next line, where it sets @F to (7, 0, 9, 3) and again evaluates $min = min($min // (), @F). Because $min has now been defined, $min // () evaluates to $min and the expression becomes $min = min(-8, 7, 0, 9, 3). At this point, -8 is still the smallest element, so $min remains -8. Finally, Perl reads in the last line, and after evaluating $min = min(-8, 5, -25, 9, 999), it finds that -25 is the smallest element in the file.

4.7 Find the numerically largest element (maximum element) on each line

```
perl -MList::Util=max -alne 'print max @F'
```

This works the same as one-liner 4.5, except that you replace min with max.

4.8 Find the numerically largest element (maximum element) over all lines

```
perl -MList::Util=max -alne '@M = (@M, @F); END { print max @M }'
```

This one-liner is similar to one-liners 4.6 and 4.7. In this one-liner, each line is auto-split and put in the @F array, and then this array is merged with the @M array. When the input has been processed, the END block executes and the maximum element is printed.

Here's another way to find the maximum element, keeping just the running maximum element instead of all elements in memory:

```
perl -MList::Util=max -alne '
  $max = max @F;
  $rmax = $max unless defined $rmax && $max < $rmax;
  END { print $rmax }
'
```

If you're using Perl 5.10 or later, you can use the // operator to shorten this one-liner:

```
perl -MList::Util=max -alne '$max = max($max // (), @F); END { print $max }'
```

This is the same as one-liner 4.6, except you replace min with max.

4.9 Replace each field with its absolute value

```
perl -alne 'print "@{[map { abs } @F]}"'
```

This one-liner first auto-splits the line using the -a option. The split fields end up in the @F variable. Next, it calls the absolute value function abs on each field with the help of the map function. Essentially, the map function applies a given function to each element of the list and returns a new list that contains the results of applying the function. For example, if the list @F is (-4, 2, 0), mapping abs over it produces the list (4, 2, 0). Finally, this one-liner prints the new list of positive values.

The @{[...]} construct, introduced in one-liner 4.4, allows you to execute the code inside the quotation marks.

4.10 Print the total number of fields on each line

```
perl -alne 'print scalar @F'
```

This one-liner forces the evaluation of @F in the scalar context, which in Perl means "the number of elements in @F." As a result, it prints the number of elements on each line.

For example, if your file contains the following lines:

```
foo bar baz
foo bar
baz
```

Running this one-liner produces the following output:

```
3
2
1
```

The first line has three fields, the second line has two fields, and the last line has one field.

4.11   Print the total number of fields on each line, followed by the line

```
perl -alne 'print scalar @F, " $_"'
```

This one-liner is the same as one-liner 4.10, with the addition of $_ at the end, which prints the whole line. (Remember that -n puts each line in the $_ variable.)

Let's run this one-liner on the same example file that I used in one-liner 4.10:

```
foo bar baz
foo bar
baz
```

Running the one-liner produces the following output:

```
3 foo bar baz
2 foo bar
1 baz
```

4.12   Print the total number of fields on all lines

```
perl -alne '$t += @F; END { print $t }'
```

Here, the one-liner keeps adding the number of fields on each line to variable $t until all lines have been processed. Next, it prints the result, which contains the number of words on all lines. Notice that you add the @F array to the scalar variable $t. Because $t is scalar, the @F array is evaluated in the scalar context and returns the number of elements it contains.

Running this one-liner on the following file:

```
foo bar baz
foo bar
baz
```

produces the number 6 as output because the file contains a total of six words.

4.13　Print the total number of fields that match a pattern

```
perl -alne 'map { /regex/ && $t++ } @F; END { print $t || 0 }'
```

This one-liner uses `map` to apply an operation to each element in the `@F` array. In this example, the operation checks to see if each element matches `/regex/`, and if it does, it increments the `$t` variable. It then prints the `$t` variable, which contains the number of fields that match the `/regex/` pattern. The `$t || 0` construct is necessary because if no fields match, `$t` wouldn't exist, so you must provide a default value. Instead of `0`, you can provide any other default value, even a string!

Looping would be a better approach:

```
perl -alne '$t += /regex/ for @F; END { print $t }'
```

Here, each element in `@F` is tested against `/regex/`. If it matches, `/regex/` returns true; otherwise it returns false. When used numerically, true converts to `1` and false converts to `0`, so `$t += /regex/` adds either `1` or `0` to the `$t` variable. As a result, the number of matches is counted in `$t`. You do not need a default value when printing the result in the `END` block because the `+=` operator is run regardless of whether the field matches. You will always get a value, and sometimes that value will be `0`.

Another way to do this is to use grep in the scalar context:

```
perl -alne '$t += grep /regex/, @F; END { print $t }'
```

Here, grep returns the number of matches because it's evaluated in the scalar context. In the list context, grep returns all matching elements, but in the scalar context, it returns the number of matching elements. This number is accumulated in `$t` and printed in the `END` block. In this case, you don't need to provide a default value for `$t` because grep returns `0` in those situations.

4.14　Print the total number of lines that match a pattern

```
perl -lne '/regex/ && $t++; END { print $t || 0 }'
```

Here, `/regex/` evaluates to true if the current line of input matches this regular expression. Writing `/regex/ && $t++` is the same as writing `if ($_ =~ /regex/) { $t++ }`, which increments the `$t` variable if the line matches the specified pattern. In the `END` block, the `$t` variable contains the total number of pattern matches and is printed; but if no lines match, `$t` is once again undefined, so you must print a default value.

4.15   Print the number π

```
perl -Mbignum=bpi -le 'print bpi(21)'
```

The `bignum` package exports the `bpi` function that calculates the π constant to the desired accuracy. This one-liner prints π to 20 decimal places. (Notice that you need to specify n+1 to print it to an accuracy of n.)

The `bignum` library also exports the constant π, precomputed to 39 decimal places:

```
perl -Mbignum=PI -le 'print PI'
```

4.16   Print the number e

```
perl -Mbignum=bexp -le 'print bexp(1,21)'
```

The `bignum` library exports the `bexp` function, which takes two arguments: the power to raise e to, and the desired accuracy. This one-liner prints the constant e to 20 decimal places.

For example, you could print the value of e^2 to 30 decimal places:

```
perl -Mbignum=bexp -le 'print bexp(2,31)'
```

As with π, bignum also exports the constant e precomputed to 39 decimal places:

```
perl -Mbignum=e -le 'print e'
```

4.17   Print UNIX time (seconds since January 1, 1970, 00:00:00 UTC)

```
perl -le 'print time'
```

The built-in time function returns seconds since the epoch. This one-liner simply prints the time.

4.18 Print Greenwich Mean Time and local computer time

```
perl -le 'print scalar gmtime'
```

The gmtime function is a built-in Perl function. When used in the scalar context, it returns the time localized to Greenwich Mean Time (GMT).

The built-in localtime function acts like gmtime, except it returns the computer's local time when it's used in the scalar context:

```
perl -le 'print scalar localtime'
```

In the array context, both gmtime and localtime return a nine-element list (known as struct tm to UNIX programmers) with the following elements:

```
($second,           [0]
$minute,            [1]
$hour,              [2]
$month_day,         [3]
$month,             [4]
$year,              [5]
$week_day,          [6]
$year_day,          [7]
$is_daylight_saving [8]
)
```

You can *slice* this list (that is, extract elements from it) or print individual elements if you need just some part of the information it contains. For example, to print H:M:S, slice the elements 2, 1, and 0 from localtime, like this:

```
perl -le 'print join ":", (localtime)[2,1,0]'
```

To slice elements individually, specify a list of elements to extract, for instance [2,1,0]. Or slice them as a range:

```
perl -le 'print join ":", (localtime)[2..6]'
```

This one-liner prints the hour, date, month, year, and day of the week.

You can also use negative indexes to select elements from the opposite end of a list:

```
perl -le 'print join ":", (localtime)[-2, -3]'
```

This one-liner prints elements 7 and 6, which are the day of the year (for example, the 200th day) and of the week (for example, the 4th day), respectively.

4.19 Print yesterday's date

```
perl -MPOSIX -le '
  @now = localtime;
  $now[3] -= 1;
  print scalar localtime mktime @now
'
```

Remember that `localtime` returns a nine-item list (see one-liner 4.18) of various date elements. The fourth element in the list is the current month's day. If you subtract 1 from this element, you get yesterday.

The `mktime` function constructs the UNIX epoch time from this modified nine-element list, and the `scalar localtime` construct prints the new date, which is yesterday. This one-liner also works in edge cases, such as when the current day is the first day of the month. You need the `POSIX` package because it exports the `mktime` function.

For example, if it's *Mon May 20 05:49:55* right now, running this one-liner prints *Sun May 19 05:49:55*.

4.20 Print the date 14 months, 9 days, and 7 seconds ago

```
perl -MPOSIX -le '
  @now = localtime;
  $now[0] -= 7;
  $now[3] -= 9;
  $now[4] -= 14;
  print scalar localtime mktime @now
'
```

This one-liner modifies the first, fourth, and fifth elements of the `@now` list. The first element is seconds, the fourth is days, and the fifth is months. The `mktime` command generates the UNIX time from this new structure, and `localtime`, which is evaluated in the scalar context, prints the date 14 months, 9 days, and 7 seconds ago.

4.21 Calculate the factorial

```
perl -MMath::BigInt -le 'print Math::BigInt->new(5)->bfac()'
```

This one-liner uses the `bfac()` function from the `Math::BigInt` module in the Perl core. (In other words, you don't need to install it.) The `Math::BigInt->new(5)` construction creates a new `Math::BigInt` object with a value of 5, after which the bfac() method is called on the newly created object to calculate the factorial of 5. Change 5 to any number you wish to find its factorial.

Another way to calculate a factorial is to multiply the numbers from 1 to *n* together:

```
perl -le '$f = 1; $f *= $_ for 1..5; print $f'
```

Here, I set $f to 1 and then loop from 1 to 5 and multiply $f by each value. The result is 120 (1*2*3*4*5), the factorial of 5.

4.22 Calculate the greatest common divisor

```
perl -MMath::BigInt=bgcd -le 'print bgcd(@list_of_numbers)'
```

Math::BigInt has several other useful math functions including bgcd, which calculates the *greatest common divisor (gcd)* of a list of numbers. For example, to find the greatest common divisor of (20, 60, 30), execute the one-liner like this:

```
perl -MMath::BigInt=bgcd -le 'print bgcd(20,60,30)'
```

To calculate the gcd from a file or user's input, use the -a command-line argument and pass the @F array to the bgcd function:

```
perl -MMath::BigInt=bgcd -anle 'print bgcd(@F)'
```

(I explained the -a argument and the @F array in one-liner 4.2 on page 30.)

You could also use Euclid's algorithm to find the gcd of $n and $m. This one-liner does just that and stores the result in $m:

```
perl -le '
  $n = 20; $m = 35;
  ($m,$n) = ($n,$m%$n) while $n;
  print $m
'
```

Euclid's algorithm is one of the oldest algorithms for finding the gcd.

4.23 Calculate the least common multiple

The *least common multiple (lcm)* function, blcm, is included in Math::BigInt. Use this one-liner to find the least common multiple of (35, 20, 8):

```
perl -MMath::BigInt=blcm -le 'print blcm(35,20,8)'
```

To find the lcm from a file with numbers, use the -a command-line switch and the @F array:

```
perl -MMath::BigInt=blcm -anle 'print blcm(@F)'
```

If you know a bit of number theory, you may recall that there is a connection between the gcd and the lcm. Given two numbers $n and $m, you know that their lcm is $n*$m/gcd($n,$m). This one-liner, therefore, follows:

```
perl -le '
  $a = $n = 20;
  $b = $m = 35;
  ($m,$n) = ($n,$m%$n) while $n;
  print $a*$b/$m
'
```

4.24 Generate 10 random numbers between 5 and 15 (excluding 15)

```
perl -le 'print join ",", map { int(rand(15-5))+5 } 1..10'
```

This one-liner prints 10 random numbers between 5 and 15. It may look complicated, but it's actually simple. int(rand(15-5)) is just int(rand(10)), which returns a random integer from 0 to 9. Adding 5 to it makes it return a random integer from 5 to 14. The range 1..10 makes it draw 10 random integers.

You can also write this one-liner more verbosely:

```
perl -le '
  $n=10;
  $min=5;
  $max=15;
  $, = " ";
  print map { int(rand($max-$min))+$min } 1..$n;
'
```

Here, all variables are more explicit. To modify this one-liner, change the variables $n, $min, and $max. The $n variable represents how many random numbers to generate, and $min-$max is the range of numbers for use in that generation.

The $, variable is set to a space because it's the output field separator for print and it's undef by default. If you didn't set $, to a space, the numbers would be printed concatenated. (See one-liner 4.4 on page 32 for a discussion of $,.)

4.25 Generate all permutations of a list

```
perl -MAlgorithm::Permute -le '
  $l = [1,2,3,4,5];
  $p = Algorithm::Permute->new($l);
  print "@r" while @r = $p->next
'
```

This one-liner uses the object-oriented interface of the module Algorithm::Permute to find all permutations of a list, that is, all ways to rearrange items. The constructor of Algorithm::Permute takes an array reference of elements to permute. In this particular one-liner, the elements are the numbers 1, 2, 3, 4, 5.

The next method returns the next permutation. Calling it repeatedly iterates over all permutations, and each permutation is put in the @r array and then printed. (Beware: The output list gets large really quickly. There are n! (n factorial) permutations for a list of n elements.)

Another way to print all permutations is with the permute subroutine:

```
perl -MAlgorithm::Permute -le '
  @l = (1,2,3,4,5);
  Algorithm::Permute::permute { print "@l" } @l
'
```

Here's what you get if you change @l to just three elements (1, 2, 3) and run it:

```
1 2 3
1 3 2
3 1 2
2 1 3
2 3 1
3 2 1
```

4.26 Generate the powerset

```
perl -MList::PowerSet=powerset -le '
  @l = (1,2,3,4,5);
  print "@$_" for @{powerset(@l)}
'
```

This one-liner uses the List::PowerSet module from CPAN. The module exports the powerset function, which takes a list of elements and returns a reference to an array containing references to subset arrays. You can install this module by running cpan List::PowerSet at the command line.

In the for loop, you call the powerset function and pass it the list of elements of @l. Next, you dereference the return value of powerset, which is a reference to an array of subsets, and then dereference each individual subset @$_ and print it.

The *powerset* is the set of all subsets. For a set of n elements, there are exactly 2^n subsets in the powerset. Here's an example of the powerset of (1, 2, 3):

```
1 2 3
2 3
1 3
3
1 2
2
1
```

4.27 Convert an IP address to an unsigned integer

```
perl -le '
  $i=3;
  $u += ($_<<8*$i--) for "127.0.0.1" =~ /(\d+)/g;
  print $u
'
```

This one-liner converts the IP address 127.0.0.1 into an unsigned integer by first doing a global match of (\d+) on the IP address. Performing a for loop over a global match iterates over all the matches, which are the four parts of the IP address: 127, 0, 0, 1.

Next, the matches are summed in the $u variable. The first bit is shifted 8 × 3 = 24 places, the second is shifted 8 × 2 = 16 places, and the third is shifted 8 places. The last is simply added to $u. The resulting integer happens to be 2130706433 (a very geeky number).

Here are some more one-liners:

```
perl -le '
  $ip="127.0.0.1";
  $ip =~ s/(\d+)\.?/sprintf("%02x", $1)/ge;
  print hex($ip)
'
```

This one-liner utilizes the fact that 127.0.0.1 can be easily converted to hex. Here, the $ip is matched against (\d+), and each IP part is transformed into a hex number with sprintf("%02x", $1) inside the s operator. The /e flag of the s operator makes it evaluate the substitution part as a Perl expression. As a result, 127.0.0.1 is transformed into 7f000001 and then interpreted as a hexadecimal number by Perl's hex operator, which converts it to a decimal number.

You can also use unpack:

```
perl -le 'print unpack("N", 127.0.0.1)'
```

This one-liner is probably as short as possible. It uses *vstring literals* (version strings) to express the IP address. A vstring forms a string literal composed of characters with the specified ordinal values. The newly formed string literal is unpacked into a number from a string in network byte order (big-endian order) and then printed.

If you have a string with an IP (rather than a vstring), you first have to convert it to byte form with the function inet_aton:

```
perl -MSocket -le 'print unpack("N", inet_aton("127.0.0.1"))'
```

Here, inet_aton converts the string 127.0.0.1 to the byte form (equivalent to the pure vstring 127.0.0.1) and then unpack unpacks it, as in the previous one-liner.

4.28 Convert an unsigned integer to an IP address

```
perl -MSocket -le 'print inet_ntoa(pack("N", 2130706433))'
```

Here, the integer 2130706433 is packed into a number in big-endian byte order and then passed to the inet_ntoa function that converts a number back to an IP address. (Notice that inet_ntoa is the opposite of inet_aton.)

You can do the same thing like this:

```
perl -le '
  $ip = 2130706433;
  print join ".", map { (($ip>>8*($_))&0xFF) } reverse 0..3
'
```

Here, the $ip is shifted 24 bits to the right and then bitwise ANDed with 0xFF to produce the first part of the IP, which is 127. Next, it's shifted 16 bits and bitwise ANDed with 0xFF, producing 0, and then shifted 8 bits and bitwise ANDed with 0xFF, producing another 0. Finally, the whole number is bitwise ANDed with 0xFF, producing 1.

The result from map { ... } is a list (127, 0, 0, 1). That list is now joined by a dot "." to produce the IP address 127.0.0.1.

You can replace join with the special variable $,, which acts as a value separator for the print statement:

```
perl -le '
  $ip = 2130706433;
  $, = ".";
  print map { (($ip>>8*($_))&0xFF) } reverse 0..3
'
```

Because reverse 0..3 is the same as 3,2,1,0, you could also write:

```
perl -le '
  $ip = 2130706433;
  $, = ".";
  print map { (($ip>>8*($_))&0xFF) } 3,2,1,0
'
```

5

WORKING WITH
ARRAYS AND STRINGS

In this chapter, we'll look at various one-liners for creating strings and arrays, for doing things like generating passwords, creating strings of certain length, finding the numeric values of characters, and creating arrays of numbers. You'll also learn about the range operator .., the x operator, the $, special variable, and the @ARGV array.

5.1   Generate and print the alphabet

```
perl -le 'print a..z'
```

This one-liner prints all letters from a to z in the English alphabet as abcdefghijklmnopqrstuvwxyz. The letters are generated by the range operator .., which, when used on strings in the list context (provided here by print), applies the magical auto-increment algorithm that advances the string to the next character. Therefore, in this one-liner, the auto-increment algorithm on the range a..z produces all letters from a to z.

I really golfed this one-liner. If I had used strict, it wouldn't have worked because of the bare words a and z. This version is more correct semantically:

```
perl -le 'print ("a".."z")'
```

Remember that the range operator .. produces a list of values. If you wish, you could print the values with comma separations by setting the $, special variable:

```
perl -le '$, = ","; print ("a".."z")'
```

The $, is the field separator. It's output by print between each field. Semantically, though, using join to separate the list of letters with a comma is more appealing because it works even when not using print directly:

```
perl -le '$alphabet = join ",", ("a".."z"); print $alphabet'
```

Here, the list a..z is joined by a comma before printing, and the output is

```
a,b,c,d,e,f,g,h,i,j,k,l,m,n,o,p,q,r,s,t,u,v,w,x,y,z
```

5.2   Generate and print all the strings from "a" to "zz"

```
perl -le 'print join ",", ("a".."zz")'
```

This one-liner uses the range operator .. again, but this time, it doesn't stop at z as in the previous one-liner. Instead, it advances z by one character, producing aa. Then it keeps going, producing ab, ac, and so on, until it hits az. At that point, it advances the string to ba, continues with bb, bc, and so on, until eventually it reaches zz.

You could also generate all strings from aa to zz by doing this:

```
perl -le 'print join ",", "aa".."zz"'
```

The output from this one-liner is

```
aa, ab, ..., az, ba, bb, ..., bz, ca, ..., zz
```

5.3　Create a hex lookup table

```
@hex = (0..9, "a".."f")
```

In this one-liner, the @hex array is filled with the numbers 0, 1, 2, 3, 4, 5, 6, 7, 8, 9 and the letters a, b, c, d, e, f. You could use this array to convert a number (in variable $num) from decimal to hex with the following base conversion formula. (This isn't a one-liner; I include it to illustrate how to use the @hex lookup array.)

```
perl -le '
  $num = 255;
  @hex = (0..9, "a".."f");
  while ($num) {
    $s = $hex[($num % 16)].$s;
    $num = int $num/16;
  }
  print $s
'
```

But surely, converting a number to hex is much easier if I use printf (or sprintf) with the %x format specifier.

```
perl -le 'printf("%x", 255)'
```

To convert the number back from hex to dec, use the hex operator:

```
perl -le '$num = "ff"; print hex $num'
```

The hex operator takes a hex string (beginning with or without 0x) and converts it to decimal.

5.4　Generate a random eight-character password

```
perl -le 'print map { ("a".."z")[rand 26] } 1..8'
```

Here, the map operator executes the code ("a".."z")[rand 26] eight times because it iterates over the range 1..8. In each iteration, the code chooses a random letter from the alphabet. When map has finished iterating, it returns the generated list of characters, and print prints it, thereby concatenating all the characters.

To also include numbers in the password, add 0..9 to the list of characters to choose from and change 26 to 36 because you now have 36 possible characters:

```
perl -le 'print map { ("a".."z", 0..9)[rand 36] } 1..8'
```

If you need a longer password, change 1..8 to 1..20 to generate one that's 20 characters long.

5.5   Create a string of specific length

```
perl -le 'print "a"x50'
```

This one-liner creates a string of 50 letters a and prints it. Operator x is the repetition operator. Here, the letter a is repeated 50 times by x50. This one-liner is handy when you need to generate a specific amount of data for debugging or other tasks. For example, if you need 1KB of data, just do this:

```
perl -e 'print "a"x1024'
```

I removed the -l argument because it would have output an additional newline symbol, producing 1025 bytes of data.

When you use the repetition operator in the list context, with a list as its first operand, you create a list with the given elements repeated, like this:

```
perl -le '@list = (1,2)x20; print "@list"'
```

This one-liner creates a list of 20 repetitions of (1, 2) that looks like (1, 2, 1, 2, 1, 2, ...). (The parentheses to the left of x make a list.)

5.6   Create an array from a string

```
@months = split ' ', "Jan Feb Mar Apr May Jun Jul Aug Sep Oct Nov Dec"
```

Here, @months is filled with values from the string containing month names. Because all month names are separated by a space, the split operator splits them and puts them in @months. As a result, $months[0] contains Jan, $months[1] contains Feb, . . . , and $months[11] contains Dec.

You could do the same thing with the qw/.../ operator:

```
@months = qw/Jan Feb Mar Apr May Jun Jul Aug Sep Oct Nov Dec/
```

The qw/.../ operator takes a space-separated string and creates an array in which each word is an array element.

Although not a one-liner per se, this is a useful, idiomatic way to create arrays that can come in handy when writing one-liners.

5.7   Create a string from the command-line arguments

```
perl -le 'print "(", (join ",", @ARGV), ")"' val1 val2 val3
```

This one-liner uses the @ARGV array, which contains all the arguments that have been passed to Perl. In this one-liner, the values passed to Perl are *val1*, *val2*, and *val3*, so @ARGV contains the strings *val1*, *val2*, and *val3*. This one-liner prints the string (*val1,val2,val3*) and would be useful, for example, to generate a SQL query.

If you're familiar with the INSERT query in SQL, you know its most basic form looks like INSERT INTO *table* VALUES (*val1, val2, val3, ...*). As you can see, this one-liner generates the VALUES part of the SQL query.

You can easily modify this one-liner to print the whole INSERT query:

```
perl -le '
  print "INSERT INTO table VALUES (", (join ",", @ARGV), ")"
' val1 val2 val3
```

Here's what the one-liner prints:

```
INSERT INTO table VALUES (val1,val2,val3)
```

5.8   Find the numeric values for characters in a string

```
perl -le 'print join ", ", map { ord } split //, "hello world"'
```

This one-liner takes the string "hello world" and splits it into a list of characters with split //, "hello world". It then maps the ord operator onto each of the characters, which returns each character's numeric value.

Finally, all of the numeric values are joined together by a comma and printed. Here's the output:

```
104, 101, 108, 108, 111, 32, 119, 111, 114, 108, 100
```

You could also do this with the unpack operator by specifying C* as the unpacking template:

```
perl -le 'print join ", ", unpack("C*", "hello world")'
```

The C in the template means "unsigned character" and * means "all characters."

To find the hexadecimal values of the characters, you could do this:

```
perl -le '
  print join ", ", map { sprintf "0x%x", ord $_ } split //, "hello world"
'
```

Here, the map operator executes sprintf "0x%x", ord $_ for every character, which returns the character's hexadecimal value prepended with '0x'. Here's the output:

```
0x68, 0x65, 0x6c, 0x6c, 0x6f, 0x20, 0x77, 0x6f, 0x72, 0x6c, 0x64
```

Similarly, to get the octal values of characters, you do this:

```
perl -le '
  print join ", ", map { sprintf "%o", ord $_ } split //, "hello world"
'
```

Here's the output:

```
150, 145, 154, 154, 157, 40, 167, 157, 162, 154, 144
```

And finally, to generate proper octal values that begin with 0, you can specify the %#o format to the sprintf function:

```
perl -le '
  print join ", ", map { sprintf "%#o", ord $_ } split //, "hello world"
'
```

And here's the output:

```
0150, 0145, 0154, 0154, 0157, 040, 0167, 0157, 0162, 0154, 0144
```

5.9   Convert a list of numeric ASCII values into a string

```
perl -le '
  @ascii = (99, 111, 100, 105, 110, 103);
  print pack("C*", @ascii)
'
```

Just as I unpacked a string into a list of values with the `C*` template in the previous one-liner, I can pack them into a string by using the same template. Here's the output from the one-liner:

```
coding
```

Another way to convert a list of numeric ASCII values into a string is to use the `chr` operator, which takes the code point value and returns the corresponding character:

```
perl -le '
  @ascii = (99, 111, 100, 105, 110, 103);
  $str = join "", map chr, @ascii;
  print $str
'
```

Here, you simply `map` the `chr` operator onto each numeric value in the `@ascii` array, which produces a list of characters that correspond to the numeric values. Next, you `join` the characters together and produce the `$str`, and then you print it out.

You can also golf this one-liner and come up with the following:

```
perl -le 'print map chr, 99, 111, 100, 105, 110, 103'
```

You can also use the `@ARGV` array and pass the ASCII values as arguments to the one-liner:

```
perl -le 'print map chr, @ARGV' 99 111 100 105 110 103
```

5.10   Generate an array with odd numbers from 1 to 100

```
perl -le '@odd = grep {$_ % 2 == 1} 1..100; print "@odd"'
```

This one-liner generates an array of odd numbers from 1 to 99 (that is, 1, 3, 5, 7, 9, 11, . . . , 99). It uses grep to evaluate the code `$_ % 2 == 1` for each element in the list `1..100` and returns only those elements for which the given code evaluates to true. In this case, the code tests to see if the remainder when dividing by 2 is 1. If it is, the number is odd, and it's put in the @odd array.

You could also write this using the fact that odd numbers have the least significant bit set and test for the least significant bit:

```
perl -le '@odd = grep { $_ & 1 } 1..100; print "@odd"'
```

The expression $_ & 1 isolates the least significant bit, and grep selects only those numbers with the least significant bit set—that is, all odd numbers.

5.11 Generate an array with even numbers from 1 to 100

```
perl -le '@even = grep {$_ % 2 == 0} 1..100; print "@even"'
```

This one-liner is almost the same as the one in 5.10, except that grep tests for the condition "is the number even (remainder after dividing by two is 0)?"

5.12 Find the length of a string

```
perl -le 'print length "one-liners are great"'
```

The length subroutine finds the length of a string.

5.13 Find the number of elements in an array

```
perl -le '@array = ("a".."z"); print scalar @array'
```

Evaluating an array in the scalar context returns its number of elements.

You could also do this by adding 1 to the last index of an array:

```
perl -le '@array = ("a".."z"); print $#array + 1'
```

Here, $#array returns the last index in @array. Because that number is one less than the number of elements in the array, you add 1 to the result to find the total number of elements in the array.

For example, say you want to find out how many text files are in the current directory. You can use @ARGV and pass the *.txt wildcard to Perl.

The shell expands the *.txt wildcard to a list of filenames that match *.txt, and Perl puts them into the @ARGV array and prints the array in the scalar context. The output will be the number of text files in the current directory:

```
perl -le 'print scalar @ARGV' *.txt
```

If your shell doesn't support filename expansion (also known as *globbing*) or if you're on Windows, you can use the diamond operator with the *.txt argument:

```
perl -le 'print scalar (@ARGV=<*.txt>)'
```

In this case, the diamond operator does the globbing and returns a list of filenames that match *.txt. Evaluating this list in the scalar context returns the number of files that matched.

6

TEXT CONVERSION AND SUBSTITUTION

In this chapter, we'll look at various one-liners that change, convert, and substitute text, including base64 encoding and decoding, URL escaping and unescaping, HTML escaping and unescaping, converting text case, and reversing lines. You'll also get to know the y, tr, uc, lc, and reverse operators and string-escape sequences.

6.1   ROT13 a string

```
perl -le '$string = "bananas"; $string =~ y/A-Za-z/N-ZA-Mn-za-m/; print $string'
```

This one-liner uses the y operator (also known as the tr operator) to do ROT13. The operators y and tr perform string transliteration. Given y/*search*/*replace*/, the y operator transliterates all occurrences of the characters found in the *search* list with the characters in the corresponding positions in the *replace* list. The y and tr operators are often mistaken for taking a regular expression, but they don't. They transliterate things and take a list of characters in both the *search* and *replace* parts.

In this one-liner, A-Za-z creates the following list of characters:

```
ABCDEFGHIJKLMNOPQRSTUVWXYZabcdefghijklmnopqrstuvwxyz
```

And N-ZA-Mn-za-m creates this list:

```
NOPQRSTUVWXYZABCDEFGHIJKLMnopqrstuvwxyzabcdefghijklm
```

Notice that in the second list the uppercase and lowercase alphabets are offset by 13 characters. Now the y operator translates each character in the first list to a character in the second list, thus performing the ROT13 operation. (One fun fact about ROT13 is that applying it twice produces the same string; that is, ROT13(ROT13(*string*)) equals *string*.)

To ROT13 the whole file *bananas.txt* and print it to the screen, just do this:

```
perl -lpe 'y/A-Za-z/N-ZA-Mn-za-m/' bananas.txt
```

You can also use Perl's -i argument to do in-place replacement of the file. For example, to ROT13 *oranges.txt* in-place, write this:

```
perl -pi.bak -e 'y/A-Za-z/N-ZA-Mn-za-m/' oranges.txt
```

This one-liner first creates a backup file called *oranges.txt.bak* and then replaces the contents of *oranges.txt* with ROT13-ed text. The .bak part of the -i command creates the backup file. You can omit the .bak part of the command if you're sure about the result, but I recommend always using -i.bak because one day you might make a mistake and mess up an important file. (I speak from experience.)

6.2   Base64-encode a string

```
perl -MMIME::Base64 -e 'print encode_base64("string")'
```

This one-liner uses the MIME::Base64 module. It exports the encode_base64 function, which takes a string and returns a base64-encoded version of it.

To base64-encode the whole file, use this:

```
perl -MMIME::Base64 -0777 -ne 'print encode_base64($_)' file
```

Here, the -0777 argument together with -n causes Perl to slurp the whole file into the $_ variable. Next, the file is base64-encoded and printed. (If Perl didn't slurp the entire file, it would be encoded line by line, and you'd end up with a mess.)

6.3   Base64-decode a string

```
perl -MMIME::Base64 -le 'print decode_base64("base64string")'
```

The MIME::Base64 module also exports the decode_base64 function, which takes a base64-encoded string and decodes it.

The entire file can be decoded similarly with

```
perl -MMIME::Base64 -0777 -ne 'print decode_base64($_)' file
```

6.4   URL-escape a string

```
perl -MURI::Escape -le 'print uri_escape("http://example.com")'
```

To use this one-liner, you need to install the URI::Escape module first by entering cpan URI::Escape in the shell. The module exports two functions: uri_escape and uri_unescape. The first function performs *URL escaping* (sometimes referred to as *URL encoding*), and the other does *URL unescaping* (or *URL decoding*). Now, to URL-escape a string, just call uri_escape($string) and you're done!

The output of this one-liner is http%3A%2F%2Fexample.com.

6.5   URL-unescape a string

```
perl -MURI::Escape -le 'print uri_unescape("http%3A%2F%2Fexample.com")'
```

This one-liner uses the uri_unescape function from the URI::Escape module to perform URL unescaping. It unescapes the output of the previous one-liner to reverse the operation.

The output of this one-liner is http://example.com.

6.6   HTML-encode a string

```
perl -MHTML::Entities -le 'print encode_entities("<html>")'
```

This one-liner uses the encode_entities function from the HTML::Entities module to encode HTML entities. For example, you can turn < and > into < and >.

6.7   HTML-decode a string

```
perl -MHTML::Entities -le 'print decode_entities("&lt;html&gt;")'
```

This one-liner uses the decode_entities function from the HTML::Entities module. For example, you can turn < and > back into < and >.

6.8   Convert all text to uppercase

```
perl -nle 'print uc'
```

This one-liner uses the uc function, which, by default, operates on the $_ variable and returns an uppercase version of the text it contains.

You could do the same thing with the -p command-line option, which enables the automatic printing of the $_ variable and modifies it in-place:

```
perl -ple '$_ = uc'
```

Or you can apply the \U escape sequence to string interpolation:

```
perl -nle 'print "\U$_"'
```

This one-liner uppercases everything that follows it (or everything up to the first occurrence of \E).

6.9   Convert all text to lowercase

```
perl -nle 'print lc'
```

This one-liner is similar to the previous one. The lc function converts the contents of $_ to lowercase.

You could also use the escape sequence \L and string interpolation:

```
perl -nle 'print "\L$_"'
```

Here, \L lowercases everything after it (or until the first instance of \E).

6.10 Uppercase only the first letter of each line

```
perl -nle 'print ucfirst lc'
```

This one-liner first lowercases the input with the lc function and then uses ucfirst to uppercase only the first character. For example, if you pass it a line that says *foo bar baz*, it produces the text *Foo bar baz*. Similarly, if you pass it a line *FOO BAR BAZ*, it lowercases the line first and then uppercases the first letter, producing *Foo bar baz* again.

You can do the same thing using escape codes and string interpolation:

```
perl -nle 'print "\u\L$_"'
```

First \L lowercases the whole line and then \u uppercases the first character.

6.11 Invert the letter case

```
perl -ple 'y/A-Za-z/a-zA-Z/'
```

This one-liner changes the case of the letters: The capital letters become lowercase letters, and the lowercase letters become capital letters. For example, the text *Cows are COOL* becomes *cOWS ARE cool*. The transliteration operator y (explained in one-liner 6.1 on page 59) creates a mapping from capital letters A-Z to lowercase letters a-z and a mapping from lowercase letters a-z to capital letters A-Z.

6.12 Title-case each line

```
perl -ple 's/(\w+)/\u$1/g'
```

This one-liner attempts to title-case a string, meaning the first letter of each word is uppercased; for example, *This Text Is Written In Title Case*. This one-liner works by matching every word with \w+ and replacing the matched word with \u$1, which uppercases the first letter of the word.

6.13 Strip leading whitespace (spaces, tabs) from the beginning of each line

```
perl -ple 's/^[ \t]+//'
```

This one-liner deletes all whitespace from the beginning of every line with the help of the substitution operator s. Given s/*regex*/*replace*/, it replaces the matched *regex* with the *replace* string. In this case, the *regex* is ^[\t]+, which means "match one or more spaces or tabs at the beginning of the string," and *replace* is empty, meaning "replace the matched part with an empty string."

The regular expression class [\t] can also be replaced by \s+ to match any whitespace (including tabs and spaces):

```
perl -ple 's/^\s+//'
```

6.14 Strip trailing whitespace (spaces, tabs) from the end of each line

```
perl -ple 's/[ \t]+$//'
```

This one-liner deletes all whitespace from the end of each line. The *regex* of the s operator says "match one or more spaces or tabs at the end of the string." The *replace* part is empty again, which means "erase the matched whitespace."

You can also achieve the same by writing:

```
perl -ple 's/\s+$//'
```

Here, you replace with [\t]+$ with \s+, as in one-liner 6.13.

6.15 Strip whitespace (spaces, tabs) from the beginning and end of each line

```
perl -ple 's/^[ \t]+|[ \t]+$//g'
```

This one-liner combines one-liners 6.13 and 6.14. It specifies the global /g flag to the s operator because you want it to delete whitespace at the beginning *and* the end of the string. If you don't specify this, it deletes whitespace only at the beginning (if there is whitespace) or only at the end (if there was no whitespace at the beginning).

You can also replace [\t]+$ with \s+ and get the same results:

```
perl -ple 's/^\s+|\s+$//g'
```

Writing \s+ is shorter than writing [\t]+. And s stands for space, which makes it easier to remember.

6.16 Convert UNIX newlines to DOS/Windows newlines

```
perl -pe 's|\012|\015\012|'
```

This one-liner substitutes the UNIX newline character \012 (LF) for the Windows/DOS newline character \015\012 (CRLF) on each line. One nice feature of s/*regex*/*replace*/ is that it can take characters other than forward slashes as delimiters. Here, it uses vertical pipes to delimit *regex* from *replace* to improve readability.

Newlines are usually represented as \n and carriage returns as \r, but across platforms, the meanings of the \n and \r sequences can vary. The UNIX newline character, however, is always available as \012 (LF), and the carriage-return character represented by \r is always available as \015 (CR). That's why you use those numeric codes: Sometimes using the flexible sequence is preferable, but not here.

6.17 Convert DOS/Windows newlines to UNIX newlines

```
perl -pe 's|\015\012|\012|'
```

This one-liner works in the opposite direction from one-liner 6.16. It takes Windows newlines (CRLF) and converts them to UNIX newlines (LF).

6.18 Convert UNIX newlines to Mac newlines

```
perl -pe 's|\012|\015|'
```

Mac OS previously used \015 (CR) as newlines. This one-liner converts UNIX's \012 (LF) to Mac OS's \015 (CR).

6.19 Substitute (find and replace) "foo" with "bar" on each line

```
perl -pe 's/foo/bar/'
```

This one-liner uses the s/*regex*/*replace*/ command to substitute the first occurrence of foo with bar on each line.

To replace all foos with bars, add the global /g flag:

```
perl -pe 's/foo/bar/g'
```

6.20 Substitute (find and replace) "foo" with "bar" on lines that match "baz"

```
perl -pe '/baz/ && s/foo/bar/'
```

This one-liner is roughly equivalent to

```
while (defined($line = <>)) {
  if ($line =~ /baz/) {
    $line =~ s/foo/bar/
  }
}
```

This expanded code puts each line into the variable $line and then checks to see if a line in that variable matches baz. If so, it replaces foo with bar in that line.

You could also write

```
perl -pe 's/foo/bar/ if /baz/'
```

6.21 Print paragraphs in reverse order

```
perl -00 -e 'print reverse <>' file
```

This one-liner uses the -00 argument discussed in one-liner 2.7 (page 14) to turn paragraph slurp mode on, meaning that Perl reads text paragraph by paragraph, rather than line by line. Next, it uses the <> operator to make Perl read the input from either standard input or files specified as arguments. Here, I've specified *file* as the argument so Perl will read *file* paragraph by paragraph (thanks to -00). Once Perl finishes reading the file, it returns all paragraphs as a list and calls reverse to reverse the order of the paragraph list. Finally, print prints the list of reversed paragraphs.

6.22 Print all lines in reverse order

```
perl -lne 'print scalar reverse $_'
```

This one-liner evaluates the reverse operator in the scalar context. In the previous one-liner, you saw that evaluating reverse in the list context reverses the whole list, that is, the order of the elements. To do the same for scalar values such as $_ that contain the whole line, you have to call reverse in the scalar context. Otherwise, it simply reverses a list with only one element, which is the same list! Once you've done that, you simply print the reversed line.

Often you can drop the $_ variable when using operators and Perl will still apply the function on the $_ variable. In other words, you can rewrite the same one-liner as

```
perl -lne 'print scalar reverse'
```

Or you can substitute -n for -p, modify the $_ variable, and set its value to reverse:

```
perl -lpe '$_ = reverse $_'
```

You can also write this as

```
perl -lpe '$_ = reverse'
```

Here, $_ is dropped because most Perl operators default to $_ when not given an argument.

6.23 Print columns in reverse order

```
perl -alne 'print "@{[reverse @F]}"'
```

This one-liner reverses the order of columns in a file. The -a command-line argument splits each line into columns at spaces and puts them in the @F array, which is then reversed and printed.

This one-liner is similar to one-liner 4.4 on page 32; I explained the @{[...]} construct there. It simply lets you run code inside of double quotes. For example, given the following input file:

```
one two three four
five six seven eight
```

the one-liner reverses the order of the columns, and the output is the following:

```
four three two one
eight seven six five
```

If the columns in your input are separated by any character other than a space, you can use the -F command-line argument to set a different delimiter. For example, given the following input file:

```
one:two:three:four
five:six:seven:eight
```

you can add the -F: command-line argument to the one-liner like this:

```
perl -F: -alne 'print "@{[reverse @F]}"'
```

and it produces this output:

```
four three two one
eight seven six five
```

Notice, however, that the : characters are missing in this output. To get them back, you need to modify the one-liner a bit and set the $" variable to ":", as shown here:

```
perl -F: -alne '$" = ":"; print "@{[reverse @F]}"'
```

This produces the expected output:

```
four:three:two:one
eight:seven:six:five
```

The $" variable changes the character that's printed between array elements when an array is interpolated within a double-quoted string.

7

SELECTIVELY PRINTING AND DELETING LINES

In this chapter, we'll examine various one-liners that print and delete certain lines. These one-liners will, for example, print repeated lines, print the shortest line in a file, and print lines that match certain patterns.

But every one-liner that prints certain lines can also be viewed as one that deletes the lines that aren't printed. For example, a one-liner that prints all unique lines deletes all repeated lines. I'll discuss only the one-liners that print something, rather than delete something, because one is always the inverse of the other.

7.1 Print the first line of a file (emulate head -1)

```
perl -ne 'print; exit' file
```

This one-liner is quite simple. Perl reads the first line into the $_ variable, thanks to the -n option, and then calls print to print the contents of the $_ variable. Then it just exits. That's it. The first line is printed and that's what you want.

You might also say that this one-liner deletes all lines except the first one. But don't worry. This particular one-liner won't delete the contents of the file unless you also specify the -i command-line argument, like this:

```
perl -i -ne 'print; exit' file
```

As I explained in Chapter 1 and in one-liner 6.1 on page 59, the -i argument edits the file in-place. In this case, all the lines in the file would be deleted except for the first. When using -i, always specify a backup extension to it, like this:

```
perl -i.bak -ne 'print; exit' file
```

This will create a backup file *file.bak* before the contents are overwritten.

You can add the -i command-line argument to any of the one-liners to change the file content. If you don't use the -i argument, the one-liners simply print the new content of the file to screen rather than modifying the file.

7.2 Print the first 10 lines of a file (emulate head -10)

```
perl -ne 'print if $. <= 10' file
```

This one-liner uses the $. special variable, which stands for "the current line number." Each time Perl reads in a line, it increments $. by 1, so clearly this one-liner simply prints the first 10 lines.

This one-liner can also be written without the if statement:

```
perl -ne '$. <= 10 && print' file
```

Here, print is called only if the Boolean expression $. <= 10 is true, and this expression is true only if the current line number is less than or equal to 10.

Another, though somewhat trickier, way to do this is with the range operator (..) in the scalar context:

```
perl -ne 'print if 1..10' file
```

The range operator in the scalar context returns a Boolean value. The operator is *bistable*, like a flip-flop, and emulates the *line-range* (comma) operator in sed, awk, and various text editors. Its value is false as long as its left operand is false. Once the left operand is true, the range operator is true until the right operand is true, after which the range operator becomes false again. As a result, this bistable operator becomes true at the first line, stays true until the tenth line, and then becomes and remains false.

A fourth option is to follow the first example in this chapter:

```
perl -ne 'print; exit if $. == 10' file
```

Here, I put a condition on exit, which is that the current line (which I just printed) is number 10.

7.3   Print the last line of a file (emulate tail -1)

```
perl -ne '$last = $_; END { print $last }' file
```

Printing the last line of a file is trickier than printing the first line, because you never know which is the last line. As a result, you always have to keep the line you just read in memory. In this one-liner, you always save the current line held in $_ into the $last variable. When the Perl program ends, it executes the code in the END block, which prints the last line read.

Here's another way to do this:

```
perl -ne 'print if eof' file
```

This one-liner uses the eof (or end-of-file) function, which returns 1 if the next read returns the end-of-file. Because the next read after the last line in the file will return the end-of-file, this one-liner does the job. The next read means that Perl will attempt to read a character from the current file, and if reading the character fails, it will signal that the end-of-file has been reached, meaning the whole file has been read. If the read succeeds, Perl secretly puts the character back in the input stream as if nothing had happened.

7.4   Print the last 10 lines of a file (emulate tail -10)

```
perl -ne 'push @a, $_; @a = @a[@a-10..$#a] if @a>10; END { print @a }' file
```

This one-liner is a bit tricky. Here, you push each line to the @a array and then replace @a with a slice of itself if the list contains more than 10 elements. The phrase @a = @a[@a-10..$#a] means "replace @a with the last 10 elements of @a." The bit @a-10 causes @a to be evaluated in the scalar context, and thus it returns the number of elements in the array minus 10. The expression $#a is the last index in the @a array. And finally, @a[@a-10..$#a] slices (returns) the last 10 elements of the array, with which it overwrites @a itself so it always contains only the last 10 elements.

For example, suppose @a contains (line1, line2, line3, line4), and you want to print the last four lines of the file. When you read the fifth line, the array becomes (line1, line2, line3, line4, line5), and the value of @a-4 is 1 because @a in the scalar context is 5. But the value of $#a is 4 because it's the last index in the array. Therefore when you take the slice @a[@a-4..$#a], it becomes @a[1..4], which drops the front element from the array, and the @a array becomes (line2, line3, line4, line5).

A simpler way to write this is with shift:

```
perl -ne 'push @a, $_; shift @a if @a>10; END { print @a }' file
```

This one-liner doesn't need to slice @a because you can guarantee that if @a > 10, then @a == 11. shift is an operator that removes the first element of an array. So in this loop, you can simply shift off the first stored line when you have more than 10 lines.

7.5   Print only lines that match a regular expression

```
perl -ne '/regex/ && print'
```

This one-liner tests to see whether the current line matches /regex/. If so, the /regex/ match succeeds and print is called.

Instead of using &&, you can also use if to reverse the /regex/ and print statements:

```
perl -ne 'print if /regex/'
```

7.6 Print only lines that do not match a regular expression

```
perl -ne '!/regex/ && print'
```

This one-liner inverts the previous one-liner. Here, I test to see that the line doesn't match /regex/ by inverting the match via the ! operator. If the line doesn't match, I call print to print the line.

You can also write this the other way around:

```
perl -ne 'print if !/regex/'
```

And you can also use unless instead of if !:

```
perl -ne 'print unless /regex/'
```

Another way to write this is to apply De Morgan's law to !/regex/ && print:

```
perl -ne '/regex/ || print'
```

7.7 Print every line preceding a line that matches a regular expression

```
perl -ne '/regex/ && $last && print $last; $last = $_'
```

This one-liner prints a line when it is above a line that matches /regex/. Let's walk through it, beginning at the last statement, $last = $_, which saves each line in the $last variable. Suppose the next line is read and it matches /regex/. Because the previous line is saved in $last, the one-liner simply prints it. The series of && means first that the regular expression must match and second that $last must be a true value. (Blank lines are still printed because they contain the newline character.)

Say you have a file with four lines:

```
hello world
magic line
bye world
magic line
```

and you want to print all lines above those that match magic. You can do this:

```
perl -ne '/magic/ && $last && print $last; $last = $_'
```

and the one-liner will print:

```
hello world
bye world
```

7.8 Print every line following a line that matches a regular expression

```
perl -ne 'if ($p) { print; $p = 0 } $p++ if /regex/'
```

Here, I set the variable $p to 1 if the current line matches the regular expression. The fact that the variable $p is 1 indicates that the next line should be printed. Now, when the next line is read in and $p is set, that line is printed and $p is reset to 0. Quite simple.

Let's say you have this four-line file:

```
science
physics
science
math
```

and you want to print all lines below those that match science. Do this:

```
perl -ne 'if ($p) { print; $p = 0 } $p++ if /science/'
```

The one-liner will print:

```
physics
math
```

If you want to write this with && and avoid using if and curly brackets, do this:

```
perl -ne '$p && print && ($p = 0); $p++ if /science/'
```

You can also be very smart about this and simplify this one-liner to the following:

```
perl -ne '$p && print; $p = /science/'
```

If the current line matches science, then variable $p is set to a true value and the next line gets printed. If the current line doesn't match science, then $p becomes undefined and the next line doesn't get printed.

7.9 Print lines that match regular expressions AAA and BBB in any order

```
perl -ne '/AAA/ && /BBB/ && print'
```

This one-liner tests to see whether a line matches two regular expressions. If a line matches /AAA/ and /BBB/, it's printed. Specifically, this one-liner prints the line *foo AAA bar BBB baz* because it contains both *AAA* and *BBB*, but it won't print the line *foo AAA bar AAA* because it doesn't contain *BBB*.

7.10 Print lines that don't match regular expressions AAA and BBB

```
perl -ne '!/AAA/ && !/BBB/ && print'
```

This one-liner is almost the same as the previous one. Here, I test to see if a line doesn't match both regular expressions. If it doesn't match /AAA/ or /BBB/, it prints.

7.11 Print lines that match regular expression AAA followed by BBB followed by CCC

```
perl -ne '/AAA.*BBB.*CCC/ && print'
```

Here, I simply chain the regular expressions *AAA*, *BBB*, and *CCC* with .*, which means "match anything or nothing at all." If *AAA* is followed by *BBB*, which is followed by *CCC*, the line prints. For example, this one-liner matches and prints strings like *123AAA880BBB222CCC*, *xAAAyBBBzCCC*, and *AAABBBCCC*.

7.12 Print lines that are at least 80 characters long

```
perl -ne 'print if length >= 80'
```

This one-liner prints all lines that are at least 80 characters long. In Perl, you can sometimes omit the parentheses () for function calls, so here I've omitted them for the length function call. In fact, the invocations length, length(), and length($_) are all the same as far as Perl is concerned.

If you don't want to count line endings, you can turn on automatic handling of line endings with -l:

```
perl -lne 'print if length >= 80'
```

This switch ensures that a blank line has zero length, whereas it usually has length 1 or 2, depending on the file format. (UNIX newlines have length 1; Windows newlines have length 2.)

7.13 Print lines that are fewer than 80 characters long

```
perl -ne 'print if length() < 80'
```

This one-liner reverses the previous one. It checks to see whether the length of a line is less than 80 characters. Again, you use -l if you don't want the line endings to be counted.

7.14 Print only line 13

```
perl -ne '$. == 13 && print && exit'
```

As I explained in one-liner 7.2 on page 70, the $. special variable stands for "the current line number." Therefore, if $. has a value of 13, this one-liner prints the line and exits.

7.15 Print all lines except line 27

```
perl -ne '$. != 27 && print'
```

As in the previous one-liner, this one checks to see whether the line number of the current line is 27. If a line is not 27, it prints; if it is, it doesn't print.

You can accomplish the same thing by reversing print and $. != 27 and using the if statement modifier—just like this:

```
perl -ne 'print if $. != 27'
```

Or you can use unless:

```
perl -ne 'print unless $. == 27'
```

7.16 Print only lines 13, 19, and 67

```
perl -ne 'print if $. == 13 || $. == 19 || $. == 67'
```

This one-liner prints only lines 13, 19, and 67. It doesn't print any other lines. Here's how it works: It calls print if the current line number, stored in the $. variable, is 13, 19, or 67. You can use any line numbers to print specific lines. For example, to print the lines 13, 19, 88, 290, and 999, you do this:

```
perl -ne 'print if $. == 13 || $. == 19 || $. == 88 || $. == 290 || $. == 999'
```

If you want to print more lines, you can put them in a separate array and then test whether $. is in this array:

```
perl -ne '
  @lines = (13, 19, 88, 290, 999, 1400, 2000);
  print if grep { $_ == $. } @lines
'
```

This one-liner uses grep to test if the current line $. is in the @lines array. If the current line number is found in the @lines array, the grep function returns a list of one element that contains the current line number and this list evaluates to true. If the current line number is not found in the @lines array, the grep function returns an empty list that evaluates to false.

7.17 Print all lines from 17 to 30

```
perl -ne 'print if $. >= 17 && $. <= 30'
```

In this one-liner, the $. variable stands for the current line number. As a result, the one-liner checks to see whether the current line number is greater than or equal to 17 and less than or equal to 30.

You can do the same thing using the flip-flop operator, which is explained in one-liner 7.2 on page 70. The flip-flop operator operates on $. when used with integers:

```
perl -ne 'print if 17..30'
```

7.18 Print all lines between two regular expressions (including the lines that match)

```
perl -ne 'print if /regex1/../regex2/'
```

This one-liner uses the flip-flop operator (explained in one-liner 7.2 on page 70). When used with integers, the operands are tested against the $. variable. When used with regular expressions, the operands are tested against the current line, stored in the $_ variable. Initially the operator returns false. When a line matches *regex1*, the operator flips and starts returning true until another line matches *regex2*. At that point, the operator returns true for the last time and then flips to the false state. From now on the operator returns false. This one-liner, therefore, prints all lines between (and including) the lines that match *regex1* and *regex2*.

7.19 Print the longest line

```
perl -ne '
  $l = $_ if length($_) > length($l);
  END { print $l }
'
```

This one-liner keeps the longest line seen so far in the $l variable. If the length of the current line $_ exceeds the length of the longest line, the value in $l is replaced with the value of the current line. Before exiting, the END block is executed, and it prints the longest line value that's held in $l.

Remember to use -l if you want to prevent the newline characters from counting toward the line length.

7.20 Print the shortest line

```
perl -ne '
  $s = $_ if $. == 1;
  $s = $_ if length($_) < length($s);
  END { print $s }
'
```

This one-liner is the opposite of the previous one. Because it's finding the shortest line and $s is not defined for the first line, you have to set its value to the first line explicitly through $s = $_ if $. == 1. Then it simply does the opposite of the previous one-liner. That is, it checks to see whether the current line is the shortest line so far and, if so, assigns it to $s.

7.21 Print all lines containing digits

```
perl -ne 'print if /\d/'
```

This one-liner uses the regular expression \d (which stands for "a digit") to see whether a line contains a digit. If so, the check succeeds, and the line is printed. For example, this line would be printed because it contains digits:

```
coding is as easy as 123
```

However, this line wouldn't be printed because it doesn't contain digits:

```
coding is as easy as pie
```

7.22 Print all lines containing only digits

```
perl -ne 'print if /^\d+$/'
```

In this one-liner, the regular expression ^\d+$ means "match a line if it contains only digits from the beginning until the end." For example, this line would be printed because it contains only digits:

```
3883737189170238912377
```

However, this line wouldn't be printed because it also contains some characters:

```
8388338 foo bar random data 999
```

You can also invert the ^\d$ regular expression and use \D:

```
perl -lne 'print unless /\D/'
```

This one-liner is great for developing your logical reasoning because it uses logical negation twice. Here, the line prints only if it does *not* contain a non-numeric character. In other words, it prints only if all the characters are numeric. (Notice that I used the -l command-line argument for this one-liner because of the newline character at the end of the line. If I didn't use -l, the line would contain the newline character—a non-numeric character—and it wouldn't be printed.)

7.23 Print all lines containing only alphabetic characters

```
perl -ne 'print if /^[[:alpha:]]+$/'
```

This one-liner checks to see whether a line contains only alphabetic characters. If so, it prints the line. The [[:alpha:]] stands for "any alphabetic character." And [[:alpha:]]+ stands for "all alphabetic characters."

7.24 Print every second line

```
perl -ne 'print if $. % 2'
```

This one-liner prints the first, third, fifth, and seventh lines (and so on). It does so because $. % 2 is true when the current line number is odd and false when the current line number is even.

7.25 Print every second line, beginning with the second line

```
perl -ne 'print if $. % 2 == 0'
```

This one-liner is like previous one, except it prints the second, fourth, sixth, and eighth lines (and so on) because $. % 2 == 0 is true when the current line number is even.

Alternatively, you can simply invert the test from the previous example:

```
perl -ne 'print unless $. % 2'
```

7.26 Print all repeated lines only once

```
perl -ne 'print if ++$a{$_} == 2'
```

This one-liner tracks the lines it has seen so far and counts the number of times it has seen the lines previously. If it sees a line a second time, it prints the line because ++$a{$_} == 2 is true. If it sees a line more than two times, it does nothing because the count for this line is greater than 2.

7.27 Print all unique lines

```
perl -ne 'print unless $a{$_}++'
```

This one-liner prints a line only if the hash value $a{$_} for that line is false. Every time Perl reads in a line, it increments $a{$_}, which ensures that this one-liner prints only never-before-seen lines.

8

USEFUL REGULAR EXPRESSIONS

In this chapter, we'll look at various regular expressions and how to use them in some handy one-liners. The regular expressions include matching IP addresses, HTTP headers, and email addresses; matching numbers and number ranges; and extracting and changing matches. I'll also share some regular expression puzzles and best practices. This chapter will be a bit different from previous ones because I'll start with a regular expression and then write a one-liner that uses it.

8.1   Match something that looks like an IP address

```
/^\d{1,3}\.\d{1,3}\.\d{1,3}\.\d{1,3}$/
```

This regular expression doesn't actually guarantee that the thing that matched is, in fact, a valid IP; it simply matches something that looks like an IP address. For example, it matches a valid IP such as 81.198.240.140 as well as an invalid IP such as 936.345.643.21.

Here's how it works. The ^ at the beginning of the regular expression is an anchor that matches the beginning of the string. Next, \d{1,3} matches one, two, or three consecutive digits. The \. matches a dot. The $ at the end is an anchor that matches the end of the string. (You use both ^ and $ anchors to prevent strings like foo213.3.1.2bar from matching.)

You can simplify this regular expression by grouping the first three repeated \d{1,3}\. expressions:

```
/^(\d{1,3}\.){3}\d{1,3}$/
```

Say you have a file with the following content and you want to extract only the lines that look like IP addresses:

```
81.198.240.140
1.2.3.4
5.5
444.444.444.444
90.9000.90000.90000
127.0.0.1
```

To extract only the matching lines, you can write this:

```
perl -ne 'print if /^\d{1,3}\.\d{1,3}\.\d{1,3}\.\d{1,3}$/'
```

which should print

```
81.198.240.140
1.2.3.4
444.444.444.444
127.0.0.1
```

One-liner 8.3 explains how to match an IP precisely, not just something that looks like an IP.

8.2   Test whether a number is in the range 0 to 255

```
/^([0-9]|[0-9][0-9]|1[0-9][0-9]|2[0-4][0-9]|25[0-5])$/
```

I like to challenge people with puzzles. One of my favorites is to ask someone to come up with a regular expression that matches a number range. Writing one is actually quite tricky if you've never done so before.

Here's how it works. A number can have one, two, or three digits. If the number has one digit, you allow it to be anything [0-9]. If it has two digits, you also let it be any combination of [0-9][0-9]. But if the number has three digits, it has to be either one hundred–something or two hundred–something. If the number is one hundred–something, 1[0-9][0-9] matches it. If the number is two hundred–something, the number is either 200 to 249 (which is matched by 2[0-4][0-9]) or it's 250 to 255 (which is matched by 25[0-5]).

Let's confirm this regular expression really matches all numbers in the range 0 to 255 and write a one-liner to do it:

```
perl -le '
  map { $n++ if /^([0-9]|[0-9][0-9]|1[0-9][0-9]|2[0-4][0-9]|25[0-5])$/ } 0..255;
  END { print $n }
'
```

This one-liner outputs 256, the total numbers in the range 0 to 255. It iterates over the range 0 to 255 and increments the $n variable for every number that matches. If the output value was less than 256, you'd know that some numbers didn't match.

Let's also make sure this one-liner doesn't match numbers above 255:

```
perl -le '
  map { $n++ if /^([0-9]|[0-9][0-9]|1[0-9][0-9]|2[0-4][0-9]|25[0-5])$/ } 0..1000;
  END { print $n }
'
```

Although there are 1001 iterations, from 0 to 1000, the final value of $n and the output should still be 256 because numbers greater than 255 should not match. If the value was greater than 256, you'd know that too many numbers matched and the regular expression was incorrect.

8.3   Match an IP address

```
my $ip_part = qr/[0-9]|[0-9][0-9]|1[0-9][0-9]|2[0-4][0-9]|25[0-5]/;

if ($ip =~ /^$ip_part\.$ip_part\.$ip_part\.$ip_part$/) {
  print "valid ip\n";
}
```

This regular expression combines the ideas from the previous two regular expressions (8.1 and 8.2) and introduces the qr/.../ operator, which lets you construct a regular expression and save it in a variable. Here, I'm saving the regular expression that matches all numbers in the range 0 to 255 in the $ip_part variable. Next, the $ip_part matches the four parts of the IP address.

You can simplify this by grouping the first three IP parts:

```
if ($ip =~ /^($ip_part\.){3}$ip_part$/) {
  print "valid ip\n";
}
```

Let's run this on the same file from one-liner 8.1. If you have this file as input:

```
81.198.240.140
1.2.3.4
5.5
444.444.444.444
90.9000.90000.90000
127.0.0.1
```

and your one-liner is

```
perl -ne '
  $ip_part = qr|([0-9]|[0-9][0-9]|1[0-9][0-9]|2[0-4][0-9]|25[0-5])|;
  print if /^($ip_part\.){3}$ip_part$/
'
```

then the output is

```
81.198.240.140
1.2.3.4
127.0.0.1
```

As you can see, only the valid IP addresses are printed.

8.4   Check whether a string looks like an email address

```
/\S+@\S+\.\S+/
```

This regular expression makes sure the string looks like an email address; it doesn't guarantee the string is an email address, however. First, it matches something that's not whitespace (\S+) up to the @ symbol; then it matches as much as possible until it finds a dot; then it matches some more.

If the matches succeed, you know the string at least looks like an email address with the @ symbol and a dot in it. For example, cats@catonmat.net matches, but cats@catonmat doesn't because the regular expression can't find the dot that's required in a fully qualified domain name.

Here's a much more robust way to see whether a string is a valid email address, using the `Email::Valid` module:

```
use Email::Valid;
print Email::Valid->address('cats@catonmat.net') ? 'valid email' : 'invalid email';
```

Here, you use the ternary operator cond ? true : false. If the cond is true, the true part executes; otherwise the false part executes. This prints valid email if the email is valid; if not, it prints invalid email.

So a one-liner would look like this:

```
perl -MEmail::Valid -ne 'print if Email::Valid->address($_)'
```

Here, if the email address is valid, you simply print it.

8.5   Check whether a string is a number

Determining whether a string is a number is difficult with a regular expression. This is a derivation of a regular expression that matches decimal numbers.

I start with Perl's \d regular expression, which matches the digits 0 through 9:

```
/^\d+$/
```

This regular expression matches one or more digits \d from the beginning of the string ^ to the end at $. But it doesn't match numbers such as +3 and -3. Let's modify the regular expression to match them:

```
/^[+-]?\d+$/
```

Here, the [+-]? means "match an optional plus or a minus before the digits." This regular expression now matches +3 and -3 but not -0.3. Let's add that:

```
/^[+-]?\d+\.?\d*$/
```

I've expanded the previous regular expression by adding \.?\d*, which matches an optional dot followed by zero or more numbers. Now we're in business. This regular expression also matches numbers like -0.3 and 0.3, though it would not match numbers such as 123,456 or .5.

A much better way to match a decimal number is to use the `Regexp::Common` module. For example, to match a decimal number, you can use $RE{num}{real} from Regexp::Common. Here's a one-liner that filters the input and prints only the decimal numbers:

```
perl -MRegexp::Common -ne 'print if /$RE{num}{real}/'
```

This one-liner also matches and prints numbers such as 123,456 and .5. How about matching positive hexadecimal numbers? Here's how:

```
/^0x[0-9a-f]+$/i
```

This one-liner matches the hex prefix 0x followed by the hex number itself. The /i flag at the end ensures the match is case insensitive. For example, 0x5af matches, 0X5Fa matches, but 97 doesn't because 97 has no hex prefix.

Better still, use $RE{num}{hex} because it supports negative numbers, decimal places, and number grouping.

How about matching octals?

```
/^0[0-7]+$/
```

Octal numbers are prefixed by 0, which is followed by the octal digits 0-7. For example, 013 matches but 09 doesn't because it's not a valid octal number. Using $RE{num}{oct} is better because it supports negative octal numbers, octal numbers with decimal places, and number grouping.

Finally, we come to binary matching:

```
/^[01]+$/
```

Binary base consists of only 0s and 1s, so 010101 matches but 210101 doesn't because 2 is not a valid binary digit.

Regexp::Common also offers a better regular expression for matching binary numbers: $RE{num}{bin}.

8.6   Check whether a word appears in a string twice

```
/(word).*\1/
```

This regular expression matches a word followed by something or nothing at all, followed by the same word. Here, (word) captures the word in group 1, and \1 refers to the contents of group 1, which is the same as writing /(word).*word/. For example, silly things are silly matches /(silly).*\1/, but silly things are boring doesn't because silly is not repeated in the string.

8.7   Increase all integers in a string by one

```
$str =~ s/(\d+)/$1+1/ge
```

Here, you use the substitution operator s to match all integers (\d+), put them in capture group 1, and then replace them with their value incremented by one: $1+1. The g flag finds all numbers in the string, and the e flag evaluates $1+1 as a Perl expression. For example, this 1234 is awesome 444 is turned into this 1235 is awesome 445.

Note that this regular expression doesn't increment floating-point numbers because it uses \d+ to match integers. To increment floating-point numbers, use the $RE{num}{real} regular expression from one-liner 8.5. Here's a sample one-liner that uses $RE{num}{real}:

```
perl -MRegexp::Common -pe 's/($RE{num}{real})/$1+1/ge'
```

If you pass this one-liner the input weird 44.5 line -1.25, it prints weird 45.5 line -0.25.

8.8   Extract the HTTP User-Agent string from HTTP headers

```
/^User-Agent: (.+)$/
```

HTTP headers are formatted as Key: Value pairs. You can easily parse such strings by instructing the regular expression engine to save the Value part in the $1 group variable. For example, if the HTTP headers contain the following:

```
Host: www.catonmat.net
Connection: keep-alive
User-Agent: Mozilla/5.0 (Macintosh; U; Intel Mac OS X 10_0_0; en-US)
Accept: application/xml,application/xhtml+xml,text/html
Accept-Encoding: gzip,deflate,sdch
Accept-Language: en-US,en;q=0.8
Accept-Charset: ISO-8859-1,utf-8;q=0.7,*;q=0.3
```

then the regular expression will extract the string Mozilla/5.0 (Macintosh; U; Intel Mac OS X 10_0_0; en-US).

8.9   Match printable ASCII characters

```
/[ -~]/
```

This regular expression is tricky and smart. To understand it, take a look at `man ascii`, and you'll see that space starts at value `0x20` and the `~` character is `0x7e`. The expression `[ -~]` defines a range of characters from the space until `~`. Because all characters between the space and `~` are printable, this regular expression matches all printable characters. This is my favorite regular expression of all time because it's quite puzzling when you first see it. What does it match? A space, a dash, and a tilde? No, it matches a range of characters from the space until the tilde!

To invert the match, place `^` as the first character in the group:

```
/[^ -~]/
```

This matches the opposite of `[ -~]`, that is, all nonprintable characters.

8.10   Extract text between two HTML tags

```
m|<strong>([^<]*)</strong>|
```

Before I explain this regular expression, let me say that it's okay to match HTML with regular expressions only for quick hacks when you need to get things done and move on. You should *never* use regular expressions to match and parse HTML in serious applications because HTML is actually a complicated language, and, in general, it can't be parsed by a regular expression. Instead, use modules like `HTML::TreeBuilder` to accomplish the task more cleanly!

This regular expression saves text between the `<strong>...</strong>` HTML tags in the `$1` special variable. The trickiest part of this one-liner is `([^<]*)`, which matches everything up to the `<` character. It's a regular expression idiom.

For example, if the HTML you're trying to match is `<strong>hello </strong>`, then this regular expression captures `hello` in the `$1` variable. However, if the HTML you're trying to match is `<strong><em>hello</em></strong>`, then this regular expression doesn't match at all because there is another HTML tag between `<strong>` and `</strong>`.

To extract everything between two HTML tags, including other HTML tags, you can write:

```
m|<strong>(.*?)</strong>|
```

This regular expression saves everything between `<strong>...</strong>` in the $1 variable. For example, if the HTML is `<strong><em>hello</em></strong>`, this regular expression sets $1 to `<em>hello</em>`. The `(.*?)` part of the regular expression matches everything between the two nearest `<strong>` and `</strong>` tags. The question mark ? in this regular expression controls its greediness.

If you want to be a good citizen and use `HTML::TreeBuilder`, then a Perl program that does the same thing would look like this:

```
use warnings;
use strict;

use HTML::TreeBuilder;

my $tree = HTML::TreeBuilder->new_from_content(
  "<strong><em>hello</em></strong>"
);
my $strong = $tree->look_down(_tag => 'strong');
if ($strong) {
  print $_->as_HTML for $strong->content_list;
}
$tree->delete;
```

Here, I created a new `HTML::TreeBuilder` instance from the given string; then I found the `<strong>` tag and dumped all the child elements of the `<strong>` tag as HTML. As you can see, although writing a program like this isn't suitable as a one-liner, it's a much more robust solution.

8.11   Replace all `<b>` tags with `<strong>`

```
$html =~ s|<(/)?b>|<$1strong>|g
```

Here, I assume that the HTML is in the variable $html. The expression `<(/)?b>` matches the opening and closing `<b>` tags, captures the optional closing tag slash in the group $1, and then replaces the matched tag with either `<strong>` or `</strong>`, depending on whether it finds an opening or closing tag.

Remember that the correct way to do this is to use `HTML::TreeBuilder` and write a proper program. You should only use this regular expression for a quick hack. Here's what a program that uses `HTML::TreeBuilder` looks like:

```
use warnings;
use strict;

use HTML::TreeBuilder;
```

```
my $tree = HTML::TreeBuilder->new_from_content("
  <div><p><b>section 1</b></p><p><b>section 2</b></p></div>
");

my @bs = $tree->look_down(_tag => 'b');
$_->tag('strong') for @bs;

print $tree->as_HTML;
$tree->delete;
```

Here, I've created the `HTML::TreeBuilder` object from the given string; next, I found all the `<b>` tags, stored them in the `@bs` array, and then looped over all `@bs` and changed their tag name to `<strong>`.

8.12 Extract all matches from a regular expression

```
my @matches = $text =~ /regex/g;
```

Here, the regular expression match is evaluated in the list context, which makes it return all matches. The matches are put in the `@matches` variable.

For example, the following regular expression extracts all integers from a string:

```
my $t = "10 hello 25 moo 30 foo";
my @nums = $text =~ /\d+/g;
```

After executing this code, `@nums` contains (`10`, `25`, `30`). You can also use parentheses to capture only part of the string. For example, here's how to capture only the values from a line containing lots of key-value pairs (such as *key=value*), separated by semicolons:

```
my @vals = $text =~ /[^=]+=([^;]+)/g;
```

This regular expression first matches the keys through `[^=]+`, then it matches the `=` character that separates the keys and values, and then it matches the values (`[^;]+`). As you can see, the value part of the regular expression is wrapped in parentheses so the values are captured.

Here's an example. Say you have a file with the following contents:

```
access=all; users=peter,alastair,bill; languages=awk,sed,perl
```

and you write this one-liner:

```
perl -nle 'my @vals = $_ =~ /[^=]+=([^;]+)/g; print "@vals"'
```

Running it outputs the following:

```
all peter,alastair,bill awk,sed,perl
```

These are the values for the access, users, and languages keys!

PERL'S SPECIAL VARIABLES

In this appendix, I summarize Perl's most commonly used special (predefined) variables, such as $_, $., $/, $\, $1, $2, $3 (and so on), $,, @F, and @ARGV, among others.

A.1   Variable $_

The $_ variable, called the *default variable*, is the most commonly used variable in Perl. Often this variable is pronounced "it" (when not pronounced "dollar-underscore"); as you read on, you'll understand why.

When using the -n and -p command-line arguments, it's (see?) where the input is stored. Also, many operators and functions act on it implicitly. Here's an example:

```
perl -le '$_ = "foo"; print'
```

Here, I place the string "foo" in the $_ variable and then call print. When given no arguments, print prints the contents of the $_ variable, which is "foo".

Similarly, $_ is used by the s/*regex*/*replace*/ and /*regex*/ operators when used without the =~ operator. Consider this example:

```
perl -ne '/foo/ && print'
```

This one-liner prints only lines that match /foo/. The /foo/ operator implicitly operates on the $_ variable that contains the current line. You could rewrite this as follows, but doing so would require too much typing:

```
perl -ne 'if ($_ =~ /foo/) { print $_ }'
```

"If it matches /foo/, print it"—you get the idea. You could also replace text in all the lines simply by calling s/foo/bar/:

```
perl -pe 's/foo/bar/'
```

Interestingly, Perl borrows the $_ variable from sed. Remember that sed has a pattern space? The $_ variable can also be called Perl's pattern space. If you wrote the previous one-liner (perl -pe 's/foo/bar/') in sed, it would look like sed 's/foo/bar/' because sed puts each line in the pattern space and the s command acts on it implicitly. Perl borrows many concepts and commands from sed.

Using $_ with the -n argument

When using the -n argument, Perl puts the following loop around your program:

```
while (<>) {
    # your program goes here (specified by -e)
}
```

The while (<>) loop reads lines from standard input or files named on the command line and puts each line into the $_ variable. You can then modify the lines and print them. For example, you can reverse the lines:

```
perl -lne 'print scalar reverse'
```

Because I'm using the -n argument here, this program becomes

```
while (<>) {
    print scalar reverse
}
```

which is equivalent to

```
while (<>) {
    print scalar reverse $_
}
```

The two programs are equivalent because many Perl functions act on $_ implicitly, which makes writing reverse and reverse $_ functionally the same thing. You need scalar to put the reverse function in the scalar context. Otherwise it's in the list context (print forces the list context) and won't reverse strings. (I explain the -n flag in great detail in one-liner 2.6 on page 12 and line reversing in one-liner 6.22 on page 67.)

Using $_ with the -p argument

When you use the -p argument, Perl puts the following loop around your program:

```
while (<>) {
    # your program goes here (specified by -e)
} continue {
    print or die "-p failed: $!\n";
}
```

The result is almost the same as for the -n argument, except that after each iteration the content of $_ is printed (through print in the continue block).

To reverse the lines as I did with -n, I can do this:

```
perl -pe '$_ = reverse $_'
```

The program now becomes:

```
while (<>) {
    $_ = reverse $_;
} continue {
    print or die "-p failed: $!\n";
}
```

I've modified the $_ variable and set it to reverse $_, which reverses the line. The continue block makes sure that it's printed. (One-liner 2.1 on page 7 explains the -p argument in more detail.)

Using $_ explicitly

The $_ variable is also often used explicitly. Here are some examples of using the $_ variable explicitly:

```
perl -le '@vals = map { $_ * 2 } 1..10; print "@vals"'
```

The output of this one-liner is 2 4 6 8 10 12 14 16 18 20. Here, I use the map function to map an expression over each element in the given list and return a new list, where each element is the result of the expression. In this case, the list is 1..10 (1 2 3 4 5 6 7 8 9 10) and the expression is $_ * 2, which means multiply each element ("it") by 2. As you can see, I'm using $_ explicitly. When the map function iterates over the list, each element is put into $_ for my convenience.

Now let's use map in a handy one-liner. How about one that multiplies each element on a line by 2?

```
perl -alne 'print "@{[map { $_ * 2 } @F]}"'
```

This one-liner maps the expression $_ * 2 onto each element in @F. The crazy-looking "@{[...]}" is just a way to execute code inside quotes. (One-liner 4.2 on page 30 explains @F, and one-liner 4.4 on page 32 explains "@{[...]}".)

Another function that explicitly uses $_ is grep, which lets you filter the elements from a list. Here's an example:

```
perl -le '@vals = grep { $_ > 5 } 1..10; print "@vals"'
```

The output of this one-liner is 6 7 8 9 10. As you can see, grep filtered elements greater than 5 from the list. The condition $_ > 5 asks, "Is the current element greater than 5?"—or, more succinctly, "Is it greater than 5?"

Let's use grep in a one-liner. How about one that finds and prints all elements on the current line that are palindromes?

```
perl -alne 'print "@{[grep { $_ eq reverse $_ } @F]}"'
```

The condition specified to the grep function here is `$_ eq reverse $_`, which asks, "Is the current element the same as its reverse?" This condition is true only for palindromes. For example, given the following input:

```
civic foo mom dad
bar baz 1234321 x
```

the one-liner outputs this:

```
civic mom dad
1234321 x
```

As you can see, all of these elements are palindromes.

You can learn even more about the `$_` variable by typing `perldoc perlvar` at the command line. The *perlvar* documentation explains all the predefined variables in Perl.

A.2   Variable $.

When reading a file, the `$.` variable always contains the line number of the line currently being read. For example, this one-liner numbers the lines in *file*:

```
perl -lne 'print "$. $_"' file
```

You can do the same thing with this one-liner, which replaces the current line with the line number followed by the same line:

```
perl -pe '$_ = "$. $_"' file
```

The `$.` variable isn't reset across files, so to number multiple files simultaneously, you write

```
perl -pe '$_ = "$. $_"' file1 file2
```

This one-liner continues numbering lines in *file2* where *file1* left off. (If *file1* contains 10 lines, the first line of *file2* is numbered 11.)

To reset the `$.` variable, you use an explicit `close` on the current file handle `ARGV`:

```
perl -pe '$_ = "$. $_"; close ARGV if eof' file1 file2
```

ARGV is a special file handle that contains the currently open file. By calling eof, I'm checking to see if it's the end of the current file. If so, close closes it, which resets the $. variable.

You can change what Perl considers to be a line by modifying the $/ variable. The next section discusses this variable.

A.3   Variable $/

The $/ variable is the input record separator, which is a newline by default. This variable tells Perl what to consider a line. Say you have this simple program that numbers lines:

```
perl -lne 'print "$. $_"' file
```

Because $/ is a newline by default, Perl reads everything up to the first newline, puts it in the $_ variable, and increments the $. variable. Next, it calls print "$. $_", which prints the current line number and the line. But if you change the value of $/ to two newlines, like $/ = "\n\n", Perl reads everything up to the first two newlines; that is, it reads text paragraph by paragraph rather than line by line.

Here's another example. If you have a file like the following, you can set $/ to :, and Perl will read the file digit by digit.

```
3:9:0:7:1:2:4:3:8:4:1:0:0:1:... (goes on and on)
```

Or if you set $/ to undef, Perl reads the entire file in a single read (called *slurping*):

```
perl -le '$/ = undef; open $f, "<", "file"; $contents = <$f>"
```

This one-liner slurps the entire file *file* in variable $contents.

You can also set $/ to reference an integer:

```
$/ = \1024
```

In this case, Perl reads the file 1024 bytes at a time. (This is also called *record-by-record reading*.)

You can also use the -0 command-line switch to provide this variable with a value, but note that you can't do the record-by-record version like this. For example, to set $/ to :, specify -0072 because 072 is the octal value of the : character.

To remember what this variable does, recall that when quoting poetry, lines are separated by /.

A.4　Variable $\

The dollar-backslash variable is appended after every `print` operation. For example, you could append a dot followed by a space ". " after each `print`:

```
perl -e '$\ = ". "; print "hello"; print "world"'
```

This one-liner produces the following output:

```
hello. world.
```

Modifying this variable is especially helpful when you want to separate printouts by double newlines.

To remember this variable, just recall that you probably want to print \n after every line. Note that for Perl 5.10 and later, the function say is available, which is like `print`, except that it always adds a newline at the end and doesn't use the $\ variable.

A.5　Variables $1, $2, $3, and so on

Variables $1, $2, $3, and so on contain the matches from the corresponding set of capturing parentheses in the last pattern match. Here's an example:

```
perl -nle 'if (/She said: (.*)/) { print $1 }'
```

This one-liner matches lines that contain the string She said: and then captures everything after the string in variable $1 and prints it.

When you use another pair of parentheses, the text is captured in variable $2, and so on:

```
perl -nle 'if (/(She|He) said: (.*)/) { print "$1: $2" }'
```

In this one-liner, first either "She" or "He" is captured in variable $1 and then anything she or he said is captured in variable $2 and printed as "$1: $2". You'll get the same number of capture variables as you have pairs of parentheses.

To avoid capturing text in a variable, use the ?: symbols inside the opening parenthesis. For example, changing (She|He) to (?:She|He):

```
perl -nle 'if (/(?:She|He) said: (.*)/) { print "Someone said: $1" }'
```

will not capture "She" or "He" in variable $1. Instead, the second pair of parentheses captures what she or he said in variable $1.

Beginning with Perl 5.10, you can use named capture groups as in (?<name>...). When you do, instead of using variables $1, $2, and so on, you can use $+{name} to refer to the group. For example, this captures "She" or "He" in the named group gender and the said text in the named group text:

```
perl -nle 'if (/(?<gender>She|He) said: (?<text>.*)/) {
  print "$+{gender}: $+{text}"
}'
```

A.6   Variable $,

The $, variable is the output field separator for print when printing multiple values. It's undefined by default, which means that all items printed are concatenated together. Indeed, if you do this:

```
perl -le 'print 1, 2, 3'
```

you get 123 printed out. If you set $, to a colon, however:

```
perl -le '$,=":"; print 1, 2, 3'
```

you get 1:2:3.

Now, suppose you want to print an array of values. If you do this:

```
perl -le '@data=(1,2,3); print @data'
```

the output is 123. But if you quote the variable, the values are space separated:

```
perl -le '@data=(1,2,3); print "@data"'
```

So the output is 1 2 3 because the array is interpolated in a double-quoted string.

A.7   Variable $"

This brings us to the $" variable: a single white space (by default) that's inserted between every array value when it's interpolated. When you write things like print "@data", the @data array gets interpolated, and the value of $" is inserted between every array element. For example, this prints 1 2 3:

```
perl -le '@data=(1,2,3); print "@data"'
```

But if you change $" to, say, a dash -, the output becomes 1-2-3:

```
perl -le '@data=(1,2,3); $" = "-"; print "@data"'
```

Recall the @{[...]} trick here. If you print "@{[...]}", you can execute code placed between the square brackets. For examples and more details, see section A.1's discussion of the $_ variable on page 95 and one-liner 4.4 on page 32.

A.8   Variable @F

The @F variable is created in your Perl program when you use the -a argument, which stands for auto-split fields. When you use -a, the input is split on whitespace characters and the resulting fields are put in @F. For example, if the input line is foo bar baz, then @F is an array ("foo", "bar", "baz").

This technique allows you to operate on individual fields. For instance, you can access $F[2] to print the third field as follows (remembering that arrays start from index 0):

```
perl -ane 'print $F[2]'
```

You can also perform various calculations, like multiplying the fifth field by 2:

```
perl -ane '$F[4] *= 2; print "@F"'
```

Here, the fifth field $F[4] is multiplied by 2, and print "@F" prints all the fields, separated by a space.

You can also use the -a argument with the -F argument, which specifies the character to split on. For example, to process the colon-separated entries in /etc/passwd entries, you write

```
perl -a -F: -ne 'print $F[0]' /etc/passwd
```

which prints the usernames from /etc/passwd.

A.9   Variable @ARGV

The @ARGV variable contains the arguments that you pass to your Perl program. For example, this prints foo bar baz:

```
perl -le 'print "@ARGV"' foo bar baz
```

When you use -n or -p flags, the arguments that you pass to your Perl program are opened one by one as files and removed from @ARGV. To access the filenames passed to your program, save them in a new variable in the BEGIN block:

```
perl -nle 'BEGIN { @A = @ARGV }; ...' file1 file2
```

Now you can use @A in your program, which contains ("*file1*", "*file2*"). If you didn't do this and you used @ARGV, it would contain ("*file2*") at first, but when *file1* was processed, it would be empty (). Be careful here!

A similar-looking variable, $ARGV, contains the filename of the file currently being read, which is "-" if the program is currently reading from the standard input.

A.10 Variable %ENV

The %ENV hash contains environment variables from your shell. This variable comes in handy when you wish to predefine some values in your script and then use these values in your Perl program or one-liner.

Say you want to use the system function to execute a program that's not in the path. You could modify the $ENV{PATH} variable and append the needed path:

```
perl -nle '
  BEGIN { $ENV{PATH} .= ":/usr/local/yourprog/bin" }
  ...
  system("yourprog ...");
'
```

This one-liner prints all environment variables from Perl:

```
perl -le 'print "$_: $ENV{$_}" for keys %ENV'
```

It loops over the keys (environment variable names) of the %ENV hash, puts each key into the $_ variable, and then prints the name followed by $ENV{$_}, which is the value of the environment variable.

B

USING PERL ONE-LINERS
ON WINDOWS

In this appendix, I'll show you how to run Perl on Windows, install a bash port on Windows, and use Perl one-liners in three different ways: from the Windows bash port, the Windows command prompt (*cmd.exe*), and PowerShell.

B.1   Perl on Windows

Before you can run Perl on Windows, you need to install Perl for Windows. My favorite Windows Perl port is Strawberry Perl (*http://strawberryperl .com/*), a Perl environment with everything you need to run and develop Perl applications on Windows. Strawberry Perl is designed to function as much as possible like the Perl environment on UNIX systems. It includes Perl binaries, the gcc compiler and related build tools, and many external libraries.

To install Strawberry Perl, download and run the installer, click through a bunch of menus a few times, and you're done. My choice for the installation directory is *c:\strawberryperl*. (Installing any UNIX software for Windows in a directory with no spaces in it is always a good idea.) Once the installation is done, the installer should put the installation directory in your path environment variable so you can run Perl from the command line right away.

Unfortunately, the Windows command line is really basic compared to the command line on UNIX systems. A UNIX system runs a real shell with well-defined command-line parsing rules, but Windows doesn't really have anything like that. The Windows command line has weird rules about how it treats certain symbols, the quoting rules aren't well defined, and the escaping rules are strange, all of which makes it difficult to run Perl one-liners. Therefore, the preferred way to run one-liners on Windows is to use a UNIX shell (such as bash) for Windows, as you'll learn in the next section.

B.2   Bash on Windows

Getting a bash shell to run on Windows is simple. I recommend win-bash (*http://win-bash.sourceforge.net/*), a stand-alone bash port for Windows that doesn't need a special environment or additional DLLs. The download is a single zip file that contains the bash shell (*bash.exe*) and a bunch of UNIX utilities (such as awk, cat, cp, diff, find, grep, sed, vi, wc, and about 100 others).

To install bash and all the utilities, simply unzip the file and you're done. My choice for the installation directory is *c:\winbash*, again with no spaces in the directory. Run *bash.exe* from *c:\winbash* to start the bash shell.

If you start *bash.exe* after you install Strawberry Perl, Perl should be available for use right away because the Strawberry Perl installer should have updated the path with the installation directory. To confirm, run **perl --version**. It should output the version of the installed Perl. If you get an error saying that perl was not found, manually append the *C:\strawberryperl\perl\bin* directory to the PATH environment variable by entering this in the command line:

```
PATH=$PATH:C:\\strawberryperl\\perl\\bin
```

Bash uses the PATH variable to find executables to run. By appending Strawberry Perl's binary directory to the PATH variable, you tell bash where to look for the perl executable.

B.3   Perl One-Liners in Windows Bash

There are some important differences between bash on Windows and UNIX. The first difference pertains to file paths. Win-bash supports both UNIX-style and Windows-style paths.

Say you install win-bash in *C:\winbash*. When you start *bash.exe,* it should map the root directory / to the current C: drive. To change the root directory to another drive, such as D:, enter **cd d:** in the bash shell. To change back to C:, enter **cd c:** in the shell. Now you can access a file such as *C:\work\report.txt* via */work/report.txt, c:/work/report.txt*, or *c:\\work\\ report.txt.*

The best thing about using win-bash is that all of the one-liners in this book should work because you're running a real shell just like in a UNIX environment! For example, to number the lines in the *C:\work\ report.txt* file (one-liner 3.1 on page 17), you can run:

```
perl -pe '$_ = "$. $_"' C:/work/report.txt
```

Or you can refer to the file as if you were in UNIX:

```
perl -pe '$_ = "$. $_"' /work/report.txt
```

Or you can use Windows-style paths:

```
perl -pe '$_ = "$. $_"' C:\\work\\report.txt
```

To avoid using double backslashes, you can single-quote the file path:

```
perl -pe '$_ = "$. $_"' 'C:\work\report.txt'
```

If the filename has spaces in it, then you always have to quote it. For example, to work with *C:\Documents and Settings\Peter\My Documents\ report.txt*, quote the entire path when passing it to a one-liner:

```
perl -pe '$_ = "$. $_"' 'C:\Documents and Settings\Peter\My Documents\report.txt'
```

Or use the UNIX-style path to the file:

```
perl -pe '$_ = "$. $_"' '/Documents and Settings/Peter/My Documents/report.txt'
```

Quoting the filename is necessary here because without it Perl thinks you're passing it a bunch of files rather than a single file with spaces in it.

B.4   Perl One-Liners in the Windows Command Prompt

If, for some reason, you can't use win-bash as recommended, you can run one-liners through the Windows command prompt (*cmd.exe*). You will need to change the one-liners in this book a bit if you're running them in the Windows command prompt because of the way Windows parses and treats the command-line arguments. Here's what to do.

First, verify that Perl is available from the command prompt. Start *cmd.exe* and enter **perl --version** in the command line. If you do this after having installed Strawberry Perl, the command should output the Perl version, and you're good to go. Otherwise, you'll have to update the PATH environment variable with the path to Strawberry Perl's binary directory:

```
set PATH=%PATH%;C:\strawberryperl\perl\bin
```

As in UNIX, the PATH variable tells the command prompt where to look for executables.

Converting One-Liners in the Windows Command Prompt

Now let's see how to convert one-liners for the command prompt, beginning with one-liner 2.1 (page 7), which double-spaces a file. In UNIX, you simply run:

```
perl -pe '$\ = "\n"' file
```

If you're running this one-liner in the Windows command prompt, however, you have to make sure that it's always wrapped in double quotes from the outside and that you've escaped any double quotes and special characters inside it. With those changes, the one-liner looks like this on Windows:

```
perl -pe "$\ = \"\n\"" file
```

This one-liner is getting ugly quickly, but you can employ a couple of Perl tricks to make it look a little nicer. First, replace double quotes inside the one-liner with the qq/.../ operator, which double-quotes anything between the slashes. Writing qq/text/ in Perl is the same as writing "text". Now you rewrite this one-liner like this:

```
perl -pe "$\ = qq/\n/" file
```

That's a little nicer. You can also change the character that the qq operator uses to separate its content. For example, the syntax qq|...| double-quotes anything between the pipes:

```
perl -pe "$\ = qq|\n|" file
```

You could even use matching parentheses or curly brackets, like this:

```
perl -pe "$\ = qq(\n)" file
```

or this:

```
perl -pe "$\ = qq{\n}" file
```

Let's see how to convert several more one-liners to Windows. How about converting an IP address to an integer (one-liner 4.27 on page 45)? In UNIX you run:

```
perl -MSocket -le 'print unpack("N", inet_aton("127.0.0.1"))'
```

On Windows, you need to change the quotes outside the one-liner to double quotes and escape the double quotes inside the one-liner:

```
perl -MSocket -le "print unpack(\"N\", inet_aton(\"127.0.0.1\"))"
```

Or you can use the qq|...| operator to avoid escaping double quotes inside the one-liner:

```
perl -MSocket -le "print unpack(qq|N|, inet_aton(qq|127.0.0.1|))"
```

For things that don't need interpolation, such as the format string N and the IP address 127.0.0.1, you can also use single quotes instead of double quotes:

```
perl -MSocket -le "print unpack('N', inet_aton('127.0.0.1'))"
```

Another trick is to use the q/.../ operator, which single-quotes any text between the slashes:

```
perl -MSocket -le "print unpack(q/N/, inet_aton(q/127.0.0.1/))"
```

Writing q/N/ and q/127.0.0.1/ is the same as writing 'N' and '127.0.0.1'.

Let's convert another one-liner from UNIX to Windows. I've expanded it to multiple lines for clarity:

```
perl -le '
  $ip="127.0.0.1";
  $ip =~ s/(\d+)\.?/sprintf("%02x", $1)/ge;
  print hex($ip)
'
```

Unfortunately, to convert this to Windows, you have to join all of the lines together (making the result less readable), and apply the new quoting rules:

```
perl -le "$ip=\"127.0.0.1\"; $ip =~ s/(\d+)\.?/sprintf(\"%02x\", $1)/ge;
print hex($ip)"
```

You can increase the readability a little by using the qq operator:

```
perl -le "$ip=qq|127.0.0.1|; $ip =~ s/(\d+)\.?/sprintf(qq|%02x|, $1)/ge;
print hex($ip)"
```

or by using single quotes:

```
perl -le "$ip='127.0.0.1'; $ip =~ s/(\d+)\.?/sprintf('%02x', $1)/ge;
print hex($ip)"
```

Symbol Challenges

You might also run into issues with the caret (^) symbol in one-liners because the Windows command prompt uses the caret as the escape symbol. To tell Windows to treat the caret symbol literally, you *usually* have to replace each caret with two carets: ^^.

Let's look at several examples that simply try to print the ^ character. Here's my first attempt:

```
perl -e "print \"^\""
```

No output! The ^ symbol disappeared. Let's try ^ twice:

```
perl -e "print \"^^\""
```

This worked! It printed the ^ symbol. Now let's try using single quotes:

```
perl -e "print '^'"
```

This also worked and printed ^, and I didn't need to enter ^ twice. Using qq/^/ also works:

```
perl -e "print qq/^/"
```

As you can see, running one-liners on Windows can be tricky because there are no uniform parsing rules for the command-line arguments. You may run into similar issues when writing one-liners with the %, &, <, >, and | symbols. If so, try preceding them with the ^ escape character so that % becomes ^%, & becomes ^&, < becomes ^<, > becomes ^>, and | becomes ^|. Or try wrapping them in the qq operator, as I discussed previously. (Better yet, install win-bash and use the one-liners through it to avoid all these issues.)

Windows File Paths

When using the Windows command prompt, you can pass filenames to one-liners in several different ways. For example, to access the file *C:\work\wrong-spacing.txt,* you can enter:

```
perl -pe "$\ = qq{\n}" C:\work\wrong-spacing.txt
```

Or you can reverse the slashes:

```
perl -pe "$\ = qq{\n}" C:/work/wrong-spacing.txt
```

If the filename contains spaces, you have to quote the path:

```
perl -pe "$\ = qq{\n}" "C:\Documents and Settings\wrong-spacing.txt"
```

For more Windows Perl usage hints, see the Win32 Perl documentation at *http://perldoc.perl.org/perlwin32.html.*

B.5   Perl One-Liners in PowerShell

Running one-liners in PowerShell is a bit different than running them in the command prompt (*cmd.exe*). The main difference is that PowerShell is a modern shell implementation with different parsing rules than the command prompt. In this section, I'll show you how to run Perl one-liners in PowerShell.

First, you need to verify that Perl works in the PowerShell environment. Run `perl --version` in the PowerShell. If the command outputs the Perl version, then Perl is available, and you should be able to run the one-liners. Otherwise, update the `Path` environment variable and append Strawberry Perl's binary directory to it by running the following command in PowerShell:

```
$env:Path += ";C:\strawberryperl\perl\bin"
```

The `Path` variable tells PowerShell where to look for executables, so when you run `perl`, it searches all the directories (separated by the ; character) for *perl.exe*.

Converting One-Liners in PowerShell

Consider one-liner 2.1 (page 7), which double-spaces a file. In UNIX, the one-liner looks like this:

```
perl -pe '$\ = "\n"' file
```

To make this one-liner work in PowerShell, you have to change three things:

- Escape the $ symbol, which PowerShell uses for variables, by adding the ` character (backtick) before it: `$.
- As with the *cmd.exe* command prompt, make sure double quotes are used on the outside of the one-liner.
- Use the `qq/.../` operator for the double quotes inside the one-liner, as explained in "Converting One-Liners in the Windows Command Prompt" on page 108. You can't just escape the double quotes with a backslash as with the command prompt, however; you must use the `qq/.../` operator.

When you put it all together, the PowerShell version of this one-liner becomes:

```
perl -pe "`$\ = qq/\n/" file
```

To specify full paths to files, use Windows-style paths. For example, to reference a file at *C:\work\wrong-spacing.txt*, enter that path directly after the one-liner:

```
perl -pe "`$\ = qq/\n/" C:\work\wrong-spacing.txt
```

If the filename or file path contains spaces, enter it like this, with double quotes around it:

```
perl -pe "`$\ = qq/\n/" "C:\Documents and Settings\wrong-spacing.txt"
```

Now for another version of the same one-liner. In UNIX the one-liner looks like this:

```
perl -pe '$_ .= "\n" unless /^$/' file
```

But in PowerShell you have to change the outer single quotes to double quotes, escape the $ symbol, and change double quotes to qq/.../ inside the one-liner:

```
perl -pe "`$_ .= qq/\n/ unless /^`$/" file
```

Now let's look at the one-liner that numbers the non-empty lines in a file (one-liner 3.2 on page 18):

```
perl -pe '$_ = ++$x." $_" if /./'
```

When converted to PowerShell, the one-liner looks like this:

```
perl -pe "`$_ = ++`$a.qq/ `$_/ if /./"
```

How about the artistic one-liner that checks if a number is prime (one-liner 4.1 on page 29)?

```
perl -lne '(1x$_) !~ /^1?$|^(11+?)\1+$/ && print "$_ is prime"'
```

In PowerShell, the one-liner looks like this:

```
perl -lne "(1x`$_) !~ /^1?`$|^(11+?)\1+`$/ && print qq/`$_ is prime/"
```

Remember the one-liner on page 46 that converts IPs to integers? Here's how it looks in UNIX:

```
perl -le '
  $ip="127.0.0.1";
  $ip =~ s/(\d+)\.?/sprintf("%02x", $1)/ge;
  print hex($ip)
'
```

And here's the same one-liner for PowerShell:

```
perl -le "
  `$ip=qq|127.0.0.1|;
  `$ip =~ s/(\d+)\.?/sprintf(qq|%02x|, `$1)/ge;
  print hex(`$ip)
"
```

One-Liners in PowerShell 3.0+

If you're running PowerShell version 3.0 or later, you can use the --% escape sequence to prevent PowerShell from doing any additional parsing.

To find out which PowerShell version you're running, enter **$PSVersionTable.PSVersion** in the shell. It should output a table like this:

```
PS C:\Users\Administrator> $PSVersionTable.PSVersion
Major  Minor  Build  Revision
-----  -----  -----  --------
3      0      -1     -1
```

This table shows that you're running PowerShell version 3.0, which has the --% escape sequence. (Older versions of PowerShell don't have this sequence, in which case you have to use the tricks I described earlier.)

When using the --% escape sequence, you don't have to escape the $ symbol. It also lets you escape the double quotes with backslashes inside the one-liner. For example, here's how the one-liner that double-spaces lines looks with the --% escape sequence:

```
perl --% -pe "$\ = \"\n\""
```

You can also use the qq/.../ operator to avoid escaping double quotes inside the one-liner:

```
perl --% -pe "$\ = qq/\n/"
```

Here's how you can write the other version of the same one-liner in PowerShell 3.0 and later:

```
perl --% -pe "$_ .= \"\n\" unless /^$/" file
```

And this is how the one-liner that numbers the lines looks:

```
perl --% -pe "$_ = ++$a.qq/ $_ / if /./"
```

Here's the one-liner that uses a regular expression to see if a number is prime:

```
perl --% -lne "(1x$_) !~ /^1?$|^(11+?)\1+$/ && print \"$_ is prime\""
```

And here's the one-liner that converts IPs to integers:

```
perl --% -le "
  $ip=\"127.0.0.1\";
  $ip =~ s/(\d+)\.?/sprintf(\"%02x\", $1)/ge;
  print hex($ip)
"
```

As you can see, running one-liners in PowerShell is quite tricky and requires several workarounds. Again, I recommend that you install win-bash as described in "Bash on Windows" on page 106 to avoid having to implement these workarounds.

C

PERL1LINE.TXT

As I was writing this book, I compiled all the one-liners in a file called *perl1line.txt*. This appendix is that file. It comes in very handy when you need to quickly look up a one-liner. You can just open *perl1line.txt* in a text editor and search for the action you want to perform. The latest version of this file can always be found at *http://www.catonmat.net/download/perl1line.txt*.

C.1   Spacing

Double-space a file

```
perl -pe '$\ = "\n"'
perl -pe 'BEGIN { $\ = "\n" }'
perl -pe '$_ .= "\n"'
```

```
perl -pe 's/$/\n/'
perl -nE 'say'
```

Double-space a file, excluding the blank lines

```
perl -pe '$_ .= "\n" unless /^$/'
perl -pe '$_ .= "\n" if /\S/'
```

Triple-space a file

```
perl -pe '$\ = "\n\n"'
perl -pe '$_ .= "\n\n"'
perl -pe 's/$/\n\n/'
```

N-space a file

```
perl -pe '$_ .= "\n"x7'
```

Add a blank line before every line

```
perl -pe 's/^/\n/'
```

Remove all blank lines

```
perl -ne 'print unless /^$/'
perl -lne 'print if length'
perl -ne 'print if /\S/'
```

Remove all consecutive blank lines, leaving only one

```
perl -00 -pe ''
perl -00pe0
```

Compress/expand all blank lines into N consecutive lines

```
perl -00 -pe '$_ .= "\n"x2'
```

Double-space between all words

```
perl -pe 's/ /  /g'
```

Remove all spacing between words

```
perl -pe 's/ +//g'
perl -pe 's/\s+//g'
```

Change all spacing between words to one space

```
perl -pe 's/ +/ /g'
```

Insert a space between all characters

```
perl -lpe 's// /g'
```

C.2 Numbering

Number all lines in a file

```
perl -pe '$_ = "$. $_"'
perl -ne 'print "$. $_"'
```

Number only non-empty lines in a file

```
perl -pe '$_ = ++$x." $_" if /./'
perl -pe '$_ = ++$x." $_" if /\S/'
```

Number and print only non-empty lines in a file (drop empty lines)

```
perl -ne 'print ++$x." $_" if /./'
```

Number all lines but print line numbers only for non-empty lines

```
perl -pe '$_ = "$. $_" if /./'
```

Number only lines that match a pattern; print others unmodified

```
perl -pe '$_ = ++$x." $_" if /regex/'
```

Number and print only lines that match a pattern

```
perl -ne 'print ++$x." $_" if /regex/'
```

Number all lines but print line numbers only for lines that match a pattern

```
perl -pe '$_ = "$. $_" if /regex/'
```

Number all lines in a file using a custom format

```
perl -ne 'printf "%-5d %s", $., $_'
```

Print the total number of lines in a file (emulate wc -l)

```
perl -lne 'END { print $. }'
perl -le 'print $n = () = <>'
perl -le 'print $n = (() = <>)'
perl -le 'print scalar(() = <>)'
perl -le 'print scalar(@foo = <>)'
perl -ne '}{print $.'
```

Print the number of non-empty lines in a file

```
perl -le 'print scalar(grep { /./ } <>)'
perl -le 'print ~~grep{/./}<>'
perl -le 'print~~grep/./,<>'
perl -lE 'say~~grep/./,<>'
```

Print the number of empty lines in a file

```
perl -lne '$x++ if /^$/; END { print $x+0 }'
perl -lne '$x++ if /^$/; END { print int $x }'
perl -le 'print scalar(grep { /^$/ } <>)'
perl -le 'print ~~grep{ /^$/ } <>'
```

Print the number of lines in a file that match a pattern (emulate grep -c)

```
perl -lne '$x++ if /regex/; END { print $x+0 }'
```

Number words across all lines

```
perl -pe 's/(\w+)/++$i.".".$1/ge'
```

Number words on each individual line

```
perl -pe '$i=0; s/(\w+)/++$i.".".$1/ge'
```

Replace all words with their numeric positions

```
perl -pe 's/(\w+)/++$i/ge'
```

C.3 Calculations

Check if a number is a prime

```
perl -lne '(1x$_) !~ /^1?$|^(11+?)\1+$/ && print "$_ is prime"'
```

Print the sum of all fields on each line

```
perl -MList::Util=sum -alne 'print sum @F'
perl -MList::Util=sum -F: -alne 'print sum @F'
```

Print the sum of all fields on all lines

```
perl -MList::Util=sum -alne 'push @S,@F; END { print sum @S }'
perl -MList::Util=sum -alne '$s += sum @F; END { print $s }'
```

Shuffle all fields on each line

```
perl -MList::Util=shuffle -alne 'print "@{[shuffle @F]}"'
perl -MList::Util=shuffle -alne 'print join " ", shuffle @F'
```

Find the numerically smallest element (minimum element) on each line

```
perl -MList::Util=min -alne 'print min @F'
```

Find the numerically smallest element (minimum element) over all lines

```
perl -MList::Util=min -alne '@M = (@M, @F); END { print min @M }'
```

```
perl -MList::Util=min -alne '
  $min = min @F;
  $rmin = $min unless defined $rmin && $min > $rmin;
  END { print $rmin }
'
```

```
perl -MList::Util=min -alne '$min = min($min // (), @F); END { print $min }'
```

Find the numerically largest element (maximum element) on each line

```
perl -MList::Util=max -alne 'print max @F'
```

Find the numerically largest element (maximum element) over all lines

```
perl -MList::Util=max -alne '@M = (@M, @F); END { print max @M }'
```

```
perl -MList::Util=max -alne '
  $max = max @F;
  $rmax = $max unless defined $rmax && $max < $rmax;
  END { print $rmax }
'
```

```
perl -MList::Util=max -alne '$max = max($max // (), @F); END { print $max }'
```

Replace each field with its absolute value

```
perl -alne 'print "@{[map { abs } @F]}"'
```

Print the total number of fields on each line

```
perl -alne 'print scalar @F'
```

Print the total number of fields on each line, followed by the line

```
perl -alne 'print scalar @F, " $_"'
```

Print the total number of fields on all lines

```
perl -alne '$t += @F; END { print $t }'
```

Print the total number of fields that match a pattern

```
perl -alne 'map { /regex/ && $t++ } @F; END { print $t || 0 }'
perl -alne '$t += /regex/ for @F; END { print $t }'
perl -alne '$t += grep /regex/, @F; END { print $t }'
```

Print the total number of lines that match a pattern

```
perl -lne '/regex/ && $t++; END { print $t || 0 }'
```

Print the number π

```
perl -Mbignum=bpi -le 'print bpi(21)'
perl -Mbignum=PI -le 'print PI'
```

Print the number e

```
perl -Mbignum=bexp -le 'print bexp(1,21)'
perl -Mbignum=e -le 'print e'
```

Print UNIX time (seconds since January 1, 1970, 00:00:00 UTC)

```
perl -le 'print time'
```

Print Greenwich Mean Time and local computer time

```
perl -le 'print scalar gmtime'
perl -le 'print scalar localtime'
```

Print yesterday's date

```
perl -MPOSIX -le '
  @now = localtime;
  $now[3] -= 1;
  print scalar localtime mktime @now
'
```

Print the date 14 months, 9 days, and 7 seconds ago

```
perl -MPOSIX -le '
  @now = localtime;
  $now[0] -= 7;
  $now[3] -= 9;
  $now[4] -= 14;
  print scalar localtime mktime @now
'
```

Calculate the factorial

```
perl -MMath::BigInt -le 'print Math::BigInt->new(5)->bfac()'
perl -le '$f = 1; $f *= $_ for 1..5; print $f'
```

Calculate the greatest common divisor

```
perl -MMath::BigInt=bgcd -le 'print bgcd(@list_of_numbers)'
perl -MMath::BigInt=bgcd -le 'print bgcd(20,60,30)'
perl -MMath::BigInt=bgcd -anle 'print bgcd(@F)'
```

```
perl -le '
  $n = 20; $m = 35;
  ($m,$n) = ($n,$m%$n) while $n;
  print $m
'
```

Calculate the least common multiple

```
perl -MMath::BigInt=blcm -le 'print blcm(35,20,8)'
perl -MMath::BigInt=blcm -anle 'print blcm(@F)'
```

```
perl -le '
  $a = $n = 20;
  $b = $m = 35;
  ($m,$n) = ($n,$m%$n) while $n;
  print $a*$b/$m
'
```

Generate 10 random numbers between 5 and 15 (excluding 15)

```
perl -le 'print join ",", map { int(rand(15-5))+5 } 1..10'
```

```
perl -le '
  $n=10;
  $min=5;
  $max=15;
  $, = " ";
  print map { int(rand($max-$min))+$min } 1..$n;
'
```

Generate all permutations of a list

```
perl -MAlgorithm::Permute -le '
  $l = [1,2,3,4,5];
  $p = Algorithm::Permute->new($l);
  print "@r" while @r = $p->next
'
```

```
perl -MAlgorithm::Permute -le '
  @l = (1,2,3,4,5);
  Algorithm::Permute::permute { print "@l" } @l
'
```

Generate the powerset

```
perl -MList::PowerSet=powerset -le '
  @l = (1,2,3,4,5);
  print "@$_" for @{powerset(@l)}
'
```

Convert an IP address to an unsigned integer

```
perl -le '
  $i=3;
  $u += ($_<<8*$i--) for "127.0.0.1" =~ /(\d+)/g;
  print $u
'
```

```
perl -le '
  $ip="127.0.0.1";
  $ip =~ s/(\d+)\.?/sprintf("%02x", $1)/ge;
  print hex($ip)
'
```

```
perl -le 'print unpack("N", 127.0.0.1)'
perl -MSocket -le 'print unpack("N", inet_aton("127.0.0.1"))'
```

Convert an unsigned integer to an IP address

```
perl -MSocket -le 'print inet_ntoa(pack("N", 2130706433))'
```

```
perl -le '
  $ip = 2130706433;
  print join ".", map { (($ip>>8*($_))&0xFF) } reverse 0..3
'
```

```
perl -le '
  $ip = 2130706433;
  $, = ".";
  print map { (($ip>>8*($_))&0xFF) } reverse 0..3
'
```

```
perl -le '
  $ip = 2130706433;
  $, = ".";
  print map { (($ip>>8*($_))&0xFF) } 3,2,1,0
'
```

C.4 Working with Arrays and Strings

Generate and print the alphabet

```
perl -le 'print a..z'
perl -le 'print ("a".."z")'
perl -le '$, = ","; print ("a".."z")'
perl -le '$alphabet = join ",", ("a".."z"); print $alphabet'
```

Generate and print all the strings from "a" to "zz"

```
perl -le 'print join ",", ("a".."zz")'
perl -le 'print join ",", "aa".."zz"'
```

Create a hex lookup table

```
@hex = (0..9, "a".."f")
```

```
perl -le '
  $num = 255;
  @hex = (0..9, "a".."f");
  while ($num) {
    $s = $hex[($num % 16)].$s;
    $num = int $num/16;
  }
  print $s
'
```

```
perl -le 'printf("%x", 255)'
perl -le '$num = "ff"; print hex $num'
```

Generate a random eight-character password

```
perl -le 'print map { ("a".."z")[rand 26] } 1..8'
perl -le 'print map { ("a".."z", 0..9)[rand 36] } 1..8'
```

Create a string of specific length

```
perl -le 'print "a"x50'
perl -e 'print "a"x1024'
perl -le '@list = (1,2)x20; print "@list"'
```

Create an array from a string

```
@months = split ' ', "Jan Feb Mar Apr May Jun Jul Aug Sep Oct Nov Dec"
@months = qw/Jan Feb Mar Apr May Jun Jul Aug Sep Oct Nov Dec/
```

Create a string from the command-line arguments

```
perl -le 'print "(", (join ",", @ARGV), ")"' val1 val2 val3
```

```
perl -le '
  print "INSERT INTO table VALUES (", (join ",", @ARGV), ")"
' val1 val2 val3
```

Find the numeric values for characters in a string

```
perl -le 'print join ", ", map { ord } split //, "hello world"'
perl -le 'print join ", ", unpack("C*", "hello world")'
```

```
perl -le '
  print join ", ", map { sprintf "0x%x", ord $_ } split //, "hello world"
'
```

```
perl -le '
  print join ", ", map { sprintf "%o", ord $_ } split //, "hello world"
'
```

```
perl -le '
  print join ", ", map { sprintf "%#o", ord $_ } split //, "hello world"
'
```

Convert a list of numeric ASCII values into a string

```
perl -le '
  @ascii = (99, 111, 100, 105, 110, 103);
  print pack("C*", @ascii)
'
```

```
perl -le '
  @ascii = (99, 111, 100, 105, 110, 103);
  $str = join "", map chr, @ascii;
  print $str
'
```

```
perl -le 'print map chr, 99, 111, 100, 105, 110, 103'
perl -le 'print map chr, @ARGV' 99 111 100 105 110 103
```

Generate an array with odd numbers from 1 to 100

```
perl -le '@odd = grep {$_ % 2 == 1} 1..100; print "@odd"'
perl -le '@odd = grep { $_ & 1 } 1..100; print "@odd"'
```

Generate an array with even numbers from 1 to 100

```
perl -le '@even = grep {$_ % 2 == 0} 1..100; print "@even"'
```

Find the length of a string

```
perl -le 'print length "one-liners are great"'
```

Find the number of elements in an array

```
perl -le '@array = ("a".."z"); print scalar @array'
perl -le '@array = ("a".."z"); print $#array + 1'
perl -le 'print scalar @ARGV' *.txt
perl -le 'print scalar (@ARGV=<*.txt>)'
```

C.5   Text Conversion and Substitution

ROT13 a string

```
perl -le '$str = "bananas"; $str =~ y/A-Za-z/N-ZA-Mn-za-m/; print $str'
perl -lpe 'y/A-Za-z/N-ZA-Mn-za-m/' file
perl -pi.bak -e 'y/A-Za-z/N-ZA-Mn-za-m/' file
```

Base64-encode a string

```
perl -MMIME::Base64 -e 'print encode_base64("string")'
perl -MMIME::Base64 -0777 -ne 'print encode_base64($_)' file
```

Base64-decode a string

```
perl -MMIME::Base64 -le 'print decode_base64("base64string")'
perl -MMIME::Base64 -0777 -ne 'print decode_base64($_)' file
```

URL-escape a string

```
perl -MURI::Escape -le 'print uri_escape("http://example.com")'
```

URL-unescape a string

```
perl -MURI::Escape -le 'print uri_unescape("http%3A%2F%2Fexample.com")'
```

HTML-encode a string

```
perl -MHTML::Entities -le 'print encode_entities("<html>")'
```

HTML-decode a string

```
perl -MHTML::Entities -le 'print decode_entities("&lt;html&gt;")'
```

Convert all text to uppercase

```
perl -nle 'print uc'
perl -ple '$_ = uc'
perl -nle 'print "\U$_"'
```

Convert all text to lowercase

```
perl -nle 'print lc'
perl -nle 'print "\L$_"'
```

Uppercase only the first letter of each line

```
perl -nle 'print ucfirst lc'
perl -nle 'print "\u\L$_"'
```

Invert the letter case

```
perl -ple 'y/A-Za-z/a-zA-Z/'
```

Title-case each line

```
perl -ple 's/(\w+)/\u$1/g'
```

Strip leading whitespace (spaces, tabs) from the beginning of each line

```
perl -ple 's/^[ \t]+//'
perl -ple 's/^\s+//'
```

Strip trailing whitespace (spaces, tabs) from the end of each line

```
perl -ple 's/[ \t]+$//'
perl -ple 's/\s+$//'
```

Strip whitespace (spaces, tabs) from the beginning and end of each line

```
perl -ple 's/^[ \t]+|[ \t]+$//g'
perl -ple 's/^\s+|\s+$//g'
```

Convert UNIX newlines to DOS/Windows newlines

```
perl -pe 's|\012|\015\012|'
```

Convert DOS/Windows newlines to UNIX newlines

```
perl -pe 's|\015\012|\012|'
```

Convert UNIX newlines to Mac newlines

```
perl -pe 's|\012|\015|'
```

Substitute (find and replace) "foo" with "bar" on each line

```
perl -pe 's/foo/bar/'
perl -pe 's/foo/bar/g'
```

Substitute (find and replace) "foo" with "bar" on lines that match "baz"

```
perl -pe '/baz/ && s/foo/bar/'
perl -pe 's/foo/bar/ if /baz/'
```

Print paragraphs in reverse order

```
perl -00 -e 'print reverse <>' file
```

Print all lines in reverse order

```
perl -lne 'print scalar reverse $_'
perl -lne 'print scalar reverse'
perl -lpe '$_ = reverse $_'
perl -lpe '$_ = reverse'
```

Print columns in reverse order

```
perl -alne 'print "@{[reverse @F]}"'
perl -F: -alne 'print "@{[reverse @F]}"'
perl -F: -alne '$" = ":"; print "@{[reverse @F]}"'
```

C.6   Selectively Printing and Deleting Lines

Print the first line of a file (emulate head -1)

```
perl -ne 'print; exit' file
perl -i -ne 'print; exit' file
perl -i.bak -ne 'print; exit' file
```

Print the first 10 lines of a file (emulate head -10)

```
perl -ne 'print if $. <= 10' file
perl -ne '$. <= 10 && print' file
perl -ne 'print if 1..10' file
perl -ne 'print; exit if $. == 10' file
```

Print the last line of a file (emulate tail -1)

```
perl -ne '$last = $_; END { print $last }' file
perl -ne 'print if eof' file
```

Print the last 10 lines of a file (emulate tail -10)

```
perl -ne 'push @a, $_; @a = @a[@a-10..$#a] if @a>10; END { print @a }' file
perl -ne 'push @a, $_; shift @a if @a>10; END { print @a }' file
```

Print only lines that match a regular expression

```
perl -ne '/regex/ && print'
perl -ne 'print if /regex/'
```

Print only lines that do not match a regular expression

```
perl -ne '!/regex/ && print'
perl -ne 'print if !/regex/'
perl -ne 'print unless /regex/'
perl -ne '/regex/ || print'
```

Print every line preceding a line that matches a regular expression

```
perl -ne '/regex/ && $last && print $last; $last = $_'
```

Print every line following a line that matches a regular expression

```
perl -ne 'if ($p) { print; $p = 0 } $p++ if /regex/'
perl -ne '$p && print && ($p = 0); $p++ if /regex/'
perl -ne '$p && print; $p = /regex/'
```

Print lines that match regular expressions AAA and BBB in any order

```
perl -ne '/AAA/ && /BBB/ && print'
```

Print lines that don't match regular expressions AAA and BBB

```
perl -ne '!/AAA/ && !/BBB/ && print'
```

Print lines that match regular expression AAA followed by BBB followed by CCC

```
perl -ne '/AAA.*BBB.*CCC/ && print'
```

Print lines that are at least 80 characters long

```
perl -ne 'print if length >= 80'
perl -lne 'print if length >= 80'
```

Print lines that are fewer than 80 characters long

```
perl -ne 'print if length() < 80'
```

Print only line 13

```
perl -ne '$. == 13 && print && exit'
```

Print all lines except line 27

```
perl -ne '$. != 27 && print'
perl -ne 'print if $. != 27'
perl -ne 'print unless $. == 27'
```

Print only lines 13, 19, and 67

```
perl -ne 'print if $. == 13 || $. == 19 || $. == 67'
```

```
perl -ne '
  @lines = (13, 19, 88, 290, 999, 1400, 2000);
  print if grep { $_ == $. } @lines
'
```

Print all lines from 17 to 30

```
perl -ne 'print if $. >= 17 && $. <= 30'
perl -ne 'print if 17..30'
```

Print all lines between two regular expressions (including the lines that match)

```
perl -ne 'print if /regex1/../regex2/'
```

Print the longest line

```
perl -ne '
  $l = $_ if length($_) > length($l);
  END { print $l }
'
```

Print the shortest line

```
perl -ne '
  $s = $_ if $. == 1;
  $s = $_ if length($_) < length($s);
  END { print $s }
'
```

Print all lines containing digits

```
perl -ne 'print if /\d/'
```

Print all lines containing only digits

```
perl -ne 'print if /^\d+$/'
perl -lne 'print unless /\D/'
```

Print all lines containing only alphabetic characters

```
perl -ne 'print if /^[[:alpha:]]+$/
```

Print every second line

```
perl -ne 'print if $. % 2'
```

Print every second line, beginning with the second line

```
perl -ne 'print if $. % 2 == 0'
perl -ne 'print unless $. % 2'
```

Print all repeated lines only once

```
perl -ne 'print if ++$a{$_} == 2'
```

Print all unique lines

```
perl -ne 'print unless $a{$_}++'
```

C.7   Useful Regular Expressions

Match something that looks like an IP address

```
/^\d{1,3}\.\d{1,3}\.\d{1,3}\.\d{1,3}$/
/^(\d{1,3}\.){3}\d{1,3}$/
```

```
perl -ne 'print if /^\d{1,3}\.\d{1,3}\.\d{1,3}\.\d{1,3}$/'
```

Test whether a number is in the range 0 to 255

```
/^([0-9]|[0-9][0-9]|1[0-9][0-9]|2[0-4][0-9]|25[0-5])$/
```

```
perl -le '
  map { $n++ if /^([0-9]|[0-9][0-9]|1[0-9][0-9]|2[0-4][0-9]|25[0-5])$/ } 0..255;
  END { print $n }
'
```

```
perl -le '
  map { $n++ if /^([0-9]|[0-9][0-9]|1[0-9][0-9]|2[0-4][0-9]|25[0-5])$/ } 0..1000;
  END { print $n }
'
```

Match an IP address

```
my $ip_part = qr/[0-9]|[0-9][0-9]|1[0-9][0-9]|2[0-4][0-9]|25[0-5]/;

if ($ip =~ /^$ip_part\.$ip_part\.$ip_part\.$ip_part$/) {
  print "valid ip\n";
}
```

```
if ($ip =~ /^($ip_part\.){3}$ip_part$/) {
  print "valid ip\n";
}
```

```
perl -ne '
  $ip_part = qr|([0-9]|[0-9][0-9]|1[0-9][0-9]|2[0-4][0-9]|25[0-5])|;
  print if /^($ip_part\.){3}$ip_part$/
'
```

Check whether a string looks like an email address

```
/\S+@\S+\.\S+/
```

```
use Email::Valid;
print Email::Valid->address('cats@catonmat.net') ? 'valid email' : 'invalid email';
```

```
perl -MEmail::Valid -ne 'print if Email::Valid->address($_)'
```

Check whether a string is a number

```
/^\d+$/
/^[+-]?\d+$/
/^[+-]?\d+\.?\d*$/
```

```
perl -MRegexp::Common -ne 'print if /$RE{num}{real}/'
perl -MRegexp::Common -ne 'print if /$RE{num}{hex}/'
perl -MRegexp::Common -ne 'print if /$RE{num}{oct}/'
perl -MRegexp::Common -ne 'print if /$RE{num}{bin}/'
```

Check whether a word appears in a string twice

```
/(word).*\1/
```

Increase all integers in a string by one

```
$str =~ s/(\d+)/$1+1/ge
perl -MRegexp::Common -pe 's/($RE{num}{real})/$1+1/ge'
```

Extract the HTTP User-Agent string from HTTP headers

```
/^User-Agent: (.+)$/
```

Match printable ASCII characters

```
/[ -~]/
```

Extract text between two HTML tags

```
m|<strong>([^<]*)</strong>|
m|<strong>(.*?)</strong>|
```

Replace all <b> tags with <strong>

```
$html =~ s|<(/)?b>|<$1strong>|g
```

Extract all matches from a regular expression

```
my @matches = $text =~ /regex/g;
```

INDEX

Numbers

-0 command-line argument, 14, 100

    -00 command-line argument, 14, 66–67

    -0777 command-line argument, 60–61

e constant, 39

π constant, 39

Symbols

<> (diamond) operator, 13, 23, 57, 66

@{[...]} construct, 32–33

@ARGV array, 53, 103–104

@array1 = (@array1, @array2) construct, 33–35

@F array, 30–31, 36, 103

}{ (eskimo operator) construct, 23–24

$1, $2, $3, ... variables, 26, 101–102

$\ variable, 8–9, 101

$, (field separator) variable, 32, 102

$" variable, 68, 102–103

$/ variable, 100

$. variable, 18, 99–100

$_ variable, 8–9, 67, 95–99

$variable = () = <> construct, 23

$variable || 0 construct, 38

$variable + 0 construct, 25

=~ operator, 30

! operator, 73

!~ operator, 30

// operator, 34

. operator, 9

.. (range) operator, 49–50, 71, 78

%ENV variable, 104

|| (logical OR) operator, 34

~~ (double bitwise negate) construct, 24, 25

A

-a command-line argument, 30–31, 103

Abigail, 29

abs (absolute value) function, 36

"action if condition" statement, 18, 20

"action unless condition" statement, 11

adding

    blank lines, 7–12

    fields (calculating sum of), 5, 30–32

    spaces, between characters, 16

addresses

    email, matching lookalikes with regular expressions, 86–87

    IP

        converting unsigned integers, to and from, 45–47

        lookalikes, matching, 83–84

        valid, matching, 85–86

Algorithm::Permute module, 44

alphabet, generating, 49–50

arguments. *See* command-line arguments

@ARGV array, 53, 103–104

ARGV file handle, 99–100

arrays. *See* lists

ASCII

    characters, printable, finding with regular expressions, 90

    numeric values, converting into strings, 55

auto-splitting, 30–31, 103

B

backup files, 2

base64 encoding, 60–61

diamond operator (<>), 13, 23, 57, 66
documentation
    perldoc, 5
    Win32 Perl, 111
DOS/Windows newlines, converting, 65
double bitwise negate ~~ construct, 24, 25

E

-e command-line argument, 2, 8
-E command-line argument, 10
e constant, 39
\E escape sequence, 62, 63
elements. *See also* fields
    maximum, 35
    minimum, 33–35
    number of, in an array, 56–57
email addresses, matching lookalikes with regular expressions, 86–87
Email::Valid module, 87
empty lines, number of, 25
encoding
    as base64, 60–61
    as HTML, 62
    URLs, 61
END block, 22–23
eof function, 71
epoch, time since, 39
escape sequences
    \E, 62, 63
    \L, 63
    \u, 63
    \U, 62
escaping
    characters, to use one-liners
        in PowerShell, 112–114
        in Windows, 108–111
    loops, with the eskimo operator }{ construct, 24
    URLs, 61
eskimo operator }{ construct, 23–24
/etc/passwd, 5, 103
Euclid's algorithm, 42
exit function, 70–71

F

@F array, 30–31, 36, 103
-F command-line argument, 31, 68
factorials, calculating, 41–42
fields. *See also* words
    absolute value, replacing with, 36
    auto-splitting, 30–31
    number of, 36–38
    separator ($, variable), 32, 102
    shuffling, 32–33
    sum of, calculating, 5, 30–32
file paths, in Windows, 107, 111
filename expansion (globbing), 57
files
    backup, 2
    number of lines in, 22–25
    numbering lines in, 17–22
    printing, first and last lines in, 70–72
    slurping, 100
    spacing, 7–12
find-and-replace
    HTML tags, 91–92
    text, 2–3, 66
flip-flop operator, 71, 78
functions. *See also* operators
    abs, 36
    close, 99–100
    defined, 34
    eof, 71
    exit, 70–71
    gmtime, 40
    grep, 24–25, 98–99
    inet_aton, 46
    inet_ntoa, 47
    join, 33, 50
    lc, 62–63
    length, 13, 56
    localtime, 40, 41
    map, 36, 98
    mktime, 41
    pack, 47, 55
    printf, 22
    push, 31
    rand, 43, 51–52
    sprintf, 54
    system, 104
    time, 39
    uc, 62
    ucfirst, 63
    unpack, 46, 54

G

gcd (greatest common divisor), 42
generating
  alphabet, 49–50
  numbers
    constants, 39
    even, 56
    odd, 55–56
    random, 43–44
  passwords, 51–52
  permutations, 44
  powerset, 45
  strings, from "a" to "zz", 50
globbing (filename expansion), 57
GMT (Greenwich Mean Time), 40
gmtime function, 40
golfing (Perl), 24
greatest common divisor (gcd), 42
Greenwich Mean Time (GMT), 40
grep function, 24–25, 98–99

H

hex lookup table, 51
hex operator, 46, 51
HTML
  encoding, 62
  tags
    extracting text between, 90–91
    replacing, 91–92
HTML::Entities module, 62
HTML::TreeBuilder module, 90–92
HTTP headers, extracting User-Agent
      string from, 89

I

-i command-line argument, 2, 60, 70
-i.bak command-line argument,
      2, 60, 70
if statement, 18, 20
inet_aton function, 46
inet_ntoa function, 47
initial capitalization, 63
int operator, 25
integers
  converting IP addresses, to and
      from, 45–47
  increasing, 89
inverting case, of letters, 63

IP addresses

converting
  to unsigned integers, 45–46
  unsigned integers to, 47
matching
  lookalikes, 83–84
  valid, 85–86
iptables, 5

J

join function, 33, 50

L

-l command-line argument, 4, 13
\L escape sequence, 63
lc function, 62–63
lcm (least common multiple), 43
least common multiple (lcm), 43
length
  creating strings by, 52
  none, 13
  printing lines by, 76, 78–79
  of strings, finding, 56
length function, 13, 56
letters. *See* characters
lines
  blank, adding or removing, 12–14
  case, converting, 62–63
  number of
    empty or non-empty, 24–25
    in a file, total, 22–24
    matching a pattern, 38
  numbering, 17–22
    with total number of
      words on, 37
    words on, 26
  order, reversing, 67
  printing
    by contents, 79–80
    every second, 80–81
    first and last, 70–72
    by length, 76, 78–79
    by matching regular
      expressions, 25, 72–75, 78
    by number, 76–77
    repeated or unique, 81
  replacing text on, 66
  spacing, 7–14
List::PowerSet module, 45

lists
  converting into strings, 55
  creating from strings, 52–53
  generating
    alphabet, 49–50
    even numbers, 56
    odd numbers, 55–56
    from regular expression
      matches, 92–93
  number of elements in, 56–57
  permutations of, 44
  powerset, 45
  slicing, 40
List::Util module, 30, 32
local time, 40
localtime function, 40, 41
logical OR operator, 34
lookup table, hex, 51
lowercase, converting to,
  62–63

M

-M command-line argument, 30–31
  -Mmodule=arg, 31
Mac OS newlines, converting to, 65
map function, 36, 98
matching. *See* regular expressions
Math::BigInt module, 41–42
maximum element, calculating, 35
MIME::Base64 module, 60–61
minimum element, calculating,
  33–35
mktime function, 41
modules
  Algorithm::Permute, 44
  bignum, 39
  Email::Valid, 87
  HTML::Entities, 62
  HTML::TreeBuilder, 90–92
  List::PowerSet, 45
  List::Util, 30, 32
  Math::BigInt, 41–42
  MIME::Base64, 60–61
  POSIX, 41
  Regexp::Common, 87–88
  Socket, 46
  URI::Escape, 61
months, days, and seconds
      ago, 41

N

-n command-line argument, 3, 12,
      96–97
newlines
  adding, 7–12
  converting for different operating
      systems, 65
non-empty lines
  numbering, 18–20
  number of, 24–25
number
  of elements, in an array, 56–57
  of fields, 36–38
  of lines, 22–25, 38
numbering
  lines, 17–22, 37
  words, 26
numbers
  constants, 39
  even, 56
  odd, 55–56
  random, 43–44
numeric
  positions, of words, 27
  values, of characters, 53–54

O

one-liners in Windows
  in bash, 107
  in PowerShell, 111–115
  in Windows command prompt,
      108–111
operating systems. *See also* Windows
  newlines, converting for, 65
operators. *See also* functions
  <> (diamond), 13, 23, 57, 66
  }{ (eskimo), 23–24
  =~ operator, 30
  ! operator, 73
  !~ operator, 30
  // operator, 34
  . operator, 9
  .. (range), 49–50, 71, 78
  || (logical OR), 34
  chr, 55
  flip-flop, 71, 78
  hex, 46, 51
  int, 25
  ord, 53–54
  q/.../, 109
  qq/.../, 108
  qr/.../, 85

operators, *continued*
    `qw/.../`, 53
    `reverse`, 67
    `say`, 10
    `scalar`, 23
    `shift`, 72
    `split`, 52
    `s/regex/replace/`, 12
    ternary, 87
    `tr`, 59–60
    `x`, 12, 52
    `y`, 59–60
OR operator, logical, 34
`ord` operator, 53–54
order, reversing, 66–68

P

`-p` command-line argument, 2, 8, 97–98
`pack` function, 47, 55
paragraphs
    order of, reversing, 66–67
    slurping, 14
passwords, generating random, 51–52
patterns. *See* regular expressions
Perl
    golfing, 24
    Strawberry, 105–106, 108
    versions, 2
    on Windows, 105–106. *See also*
           Windows
`perldoc`, 5
permutations, of lists, 44
π constant, 39
`POSIX` module, 41
powerset, generating, 45
PowerShell, 111–115
prime, checking if a number is, 29–30
`printf` function, 22
printing
    fields, number of, 36–38
    lines
        by contents, 79–80
        every second, 80–81
        first and last, 70–72
        by length, 76, 78–79
        by matching regular
           expressions, 25, 72–75, 78
        non-empty, 18–20
        by number, 76–77
        number of, 22–25, 38
        repeated or unique, 81
`push` function, 31

Q

`q/.../` operator, 109
`qq/.../` operator, 108
`qr/.../` operator, 85
`qw/.../` operator, 53

R

`rand` function, 43, 51–52
random
    numbers, generating, 43–44
    passwords, generating, 51–52
range, calculating whether a number
    is in, 84–85
range operator, 49–50, 71
`Regexp::Common` module, 87–88
regular expressions
    ASCII characters, to match
        printable, 90
    email addresses, to match
        lookalikes, 86–87
    HTML tags
        to extract text between, 90–91
        to replace, 91–92
    IP addresses, and lookalikes, to
        match, 83–86
    lines matching
        to number and print, 21
        number of, 38
        to print, 25, 72–75, 78–80
    listing all matches, 92–93
    range, to test whether a number
        is in, 84–85
removing. *See* deleting
repeated
    lines, 81
    words, 88
replacing
    HTML tags, 91–92
    text, 2–3, 66
`reverse` operator, 67
ROT13, a string, 59–60

S

`say` operator, 10
`scalar` operator, 23
`shift` operator, 72
shuffling fields (words), 32–33
slicing, lists, 40
slurping, 14, 100
`Socket` module, 46

spacing
of characters, 16
of lines, 7–14
of words, 15–16
splitting, auto-, 30–31, 103
split operator, 52
sprintf function, 54
s/regex/replace/ operator, 12
Strawberry Perl, 105–106, 108
strings
arrays, creating from, 52–53
base64 encoding, 60–61
case, converting, 62–63
characters, numeric values of,
53–54
email addresses, and lookalikes,
86–87
generating
from "a" to "zz", 50
alphabet, 49–50
from ASCII values, 55
from command-line
arguments, 53
by length, 52
passwords, random, 51–52
HTML encoding, 62
integers, increasing, 89
IP addresses, and lookalikes, 83–86
length, finding, 56
numbers, checking if, 87–88
numeric values, of characters,
53–54
order, reversing, 66–68
ROT13, 59–60
shuffling fields (words), 32–33
spacing, 15–16
URL escaping, 61
with words appearing twice, 88
stripping whitespace, 64–65
substituting
HTML tags, 91–92
text, 2–3, 66
sum (of fields), calculating, 5, 30–32
system function, 104

T

ternary operator, 87
text. *See* files; lines; words
There's More Than One Way To Do It
(TIMTOWTDI), 14

time
date, 4, 40, 41
Greenwich Mean Time (GMT), 40
local, 40
UNIX, 39
time function, 39
@TimToady (Larry Wall), 14
TIMTOWTDI (There's More Than
One Way To Do It), 14
title case, converting to, 63
tr operator, 59–60

U

\u escape sequence, 63
\U escape sequence, 62
uc function, 62
ucfirst function, 63
unescaping, URLs, 61
unique lines, 81
UNIX
newlines, converting, 65
time, 39
unless statement, 11
unpack function, 46, 54
unsigned integers, converting IP
addresses to and from,
45–47
uppercase, converting to, 62–63
URI::Escape module, 61
URL-escaping, 61
usernames, listing from */etc/passwd*,
5, 103

V

valid IP addresses, matching, 85–86
values, of characters, 53–54
variables
@ARGV, 53, 103–104
@F, 30–31, 36, 103
$1, $2, $3, … variables, 26, 101–102
$\ variable, 8–9, 101
$, (field separator), 32, 102
$" variable, 68, 102–103
$/ variable, 100
$. variable, 18, 99–100
$_ variable, 8–9, 67, 95–99
%ENV, 104
v-string (version string) literal, 64

W

Wall, Larry, 14
whitespace, stripping, 64–65
win-bash (*bash.exe*), 106, 107
Windows
    bash on, 106
    bash.exe (win-bash), 106, 107
    cmd.exe, 108
    command prompt, 108–111
    file paths
        bash, 107
        command prompt, 111
        PowerShell, 112
    newlines, 65
    one-liners
        in bash, 107
        in PowerShell, 111–115
        in Windows command prompt,
            108–111
    Perl on, 105–106
    Strawberry Perl, 105–106
    win-bash, 106, 107

words. *See also* fields
    number of, on a line, 36–37
    numbering, on a line, 26
    numeric positions of, 27
    passwords, generating random,
        51–52
    repeated, 88
    shuffling, 32–33
    spacing of, 15–16

X

x operator, 12, 52

Y

y operator, 59–60
yesterday's date, 41

The Electronic Frontier Foundation (EFF) is the leading organization defending civil liberties in the digital world. We defend free speech on the Internet, fight illegal surveillance, promote the rights of innovators to develop new digital technologies, and work to ensure that the rights and freedoms we enjoy are enhanced — rather than eroded — as our use of technology grows.

EFF.ORG

ELECTRONIC FRONTIER FOUNDATION

Protecting Rights and Promoting Freedom on the Electronic Frontier